DANNY ORLIS
and the
FOOTBALL FEUD

by

BERNARD PALMER

MOODY PRESS · CHICAGO

©, 1971, by
THE MOODY BIBLE INSTITUTE
OF CHICAGO

Printed in the United States of America

Contents

CHAPTER		PAGE
1	Football Tryouts	7
2	Sandy's Problem	17
3	Ballcarrier Del	27
4	Jealousy	37
5	Drunken Quarrel	47
6	Brotherly Feud	55
7	Divorce	66
8	Alex's Counseling	76
9	New Insight for DeeDee	87
10	Passing the Buck	98
11	Another Chance	111
12	Victory	118

1

Football Tryouts

DANNY ORLIS flew up to Angle Inlet for his family a few days before school started the first of September. He wanted to stay with his parents and visit, but there wasn't time for that. He talked with his dad for a few minutes, and then kissed his mother good-bye before setting out for Fairview with his passengers.

The afternoon was beautiful for flying, with a pleasant summer sun and just enough breeze to rumple the mirrored surface of the lake and break the seal of flat water with the floats of the Cessna aircraft. He rocked the plane up on the step, gathered speed, and got off with a short run. Banking to come back over the house again, he climbed steadily as he headed across the Big Traverse of the Lake of the Woods in the direction of Fairview, Minnesota.

He was enjoying every moment of the flight, but the Davis triplets scarcely noticed the beauty that was all about them, so excited were they at the prospect of getting back to Fairview and the kids at school. Each was thinking of something different. DeeDee wondered about Sandy Cole and how she had gotten along that summer with her folks.

Del, holding his pet crow, Blackie, on his lap, was thinking about his pet deer, Jumper, and Barney Aubichon, his Indian friend. The first thing he was going to do when he got home was to saddle his horse and ride out to see old Barney. His friend would be interested in hearing what had happened at the Angle that summer. He'd get a real charge out of all the trouble Blackie had caused Mr. and Mrs. Orlis and Del and Doug. Del was anxious to know how Barney was getting along too. He hadn't realized until now how much he missed the aging Cree.

Doug, however, was thinking of none of those things. His chief concern was football practice. It ought to be starting soon, if it hadn't already. He hoped that it hadn't. He didn't like the idea of getting a later start than the rest of the squad. That could cause a guy to lose his position. One thing in his favor was the fact that he was in good condition. Working on the Angle had seen to that.

"What about football practice, Danny?" he asked. "Has it started yet?"

"I think they've been at it about a week. I've

Football Tryouts

seen them on the practice field doing calisthenics as I've gone by on my way to the airport."

Doug frowned, fingering the lobe of his ear thoughtfully. He had had a lot of fun at the Angle that summer, but at the moment he was wishing Danny had come after them a couple of weeks earlier. It would have made it a lot easier for him to get a starting position. Actually, this year would be worse for him that way than any other because there was a new coach to get acquainted with. He lapsed into silence for the rest of the trip.

They were almost home when Danny turned his attention to Del. "I saw the assistant football coach on the street the other day. He was asking about you."

Question marks glinted in the boy's eyes. "Me? Why would he ask about me?"

"He wanted to know if there was any chance in my being able to persuade you to go out for football this season."

Del pulled in a deep breath and expelled the air with a rush. "You've got to be kidding."

"I'm giving you the straight goods. He said that he's seen you run and figured that you were fast enough to be able to help the team a great deal, if you could just be persuaded to go out for the squad."

The boy laughed. "He'd soon change his mind if he saw *me* trying to play football."

Doug, who had been only half listening to the

conversation, spoke up. "That's a bunch of baloney. You could do a good job of playing football and have a lot of fun besides—if you'd just have confidence enough in yourself to try."

Del reached a finger into Blackie's cage and stroked his pet crow's head lovingly. Going out for football might be all right, but it would take a lot of time. He wouldn't be able to work with Blackie and Jumper or go to see Barney as much as he wanted to.

"Sorry," he said, "but I've got too much to do."

Doug snorted his indignation. "I don't know why you have to be so stubborn. You don't have a bit of school spirit. You don't care whether Fairview wins or not!"

Danny changed the subject quickly. He didn't know why the two brothers had to be so different from one another. They didn't act as though they were even members of the same family.

Del slouched in the seat, dark eyes flashing. It wouldn't do any good for him to go out for the football team, in spite of what anybody said. He'd never be able to survive the first cut in the squad. But, the more he thought about it, the more interesting it became. It would be something to do and, even if he didn't make the team, he would get Doug off his back. That would be one accomplishment.

By the time they landed at Fairview on the river that skirted the airport, he was seriously considering

Football Tryouts

trying out for the team, or at least talking to the coach about it. It wouldn't do any harm to find out what Mr. McKenzie had to say.

* * *

Although Alex Smith had signed a contract to coach at Fairview months before, he and his wife, Robin, had just moved back and still weren't settled in their new apartment. He had graduated from the university in June and was going to be the new coach and guidance counselor at his home school, but he went ahead with plans to take two courses in summer school at the university. He was already starting work on his master's degree.

Robin was much more excited than Alex about moving back to their old hometown. He had to admit there was a certain amount of satisfaction in being a coach at Fairview after having quit school for a time, but Robin found it exciting for other reasons. She was happy to be back in the town where her parents and friends lived.

At the end of the first week of football practice he came home, bubbling about his team's prospects.

"I tell you Robin, I've got some kids who are going to make some of the regulars on the first string last year start to scramble to hold onto their positions."

"That's good," she answered. She really didn't care much about football, but she had long since learned that she ought to try to be excited about Alex's football squads.

"McKenzie thinks we've got a good prospect in one of the Davis triplets who lives with Orlis."

She looked up from the stove.

"Doug?" She remembered reading about him playing basketball the year before and assumed he was the one who had attracted the assistant coach's interest.

Alex shook his head. "Doug's all right, according to McKenzie, but he says the guy to watch is Del. He says he can run like chain lightning and is shifty on his feet. He thinks we can make a tremendous ballcarrier out of him, if he can just be persuaded to go out for football."

"That shouldn't be so hard, should it?"

"That's what I thought, but I guess he couldn't care less about competitive sports."

* * *

The morning school started Del went down to the assistant coach's office.

"Danny said you wanted to talk to me, Mr. McKenzie," he said, neglecting to add that his foster father had mentioned the reason for the interview.

McKenzie picked up the ball-point pen on his desk and twisted it between his fingers. "That's right. I did tell Danny that I wanted to talk to you."

There was a brief uncomfortable silence. Then McKenzie leaned forward and lowered his voice as

Football Tryouts 13

though he was about to reveal some secret information. "Tell me, have you ever thought about going out for football?"

"Once in a while." Del didn't know why, but just mentioning the sport caused his resistance to it to flame higher.

"I don't know whether you know it or not, but we've got a new coach this year, a hometown fellow."

"Danny mentioned that Alex Smith is going to be our coach this year."

"And he really knows football. I think he's one of the most knowledgeable coaches I've worked with."

Del waited for him to continue.

"We've got the biggest squad this year that we've ever had so the competition for each position is going to be stiff, but there's always room for a fellow who really puts out, who's willing to run faster and block harder than anyone else."

Del wasn't exactly sure what Coach McKenzie was trying to say, but he thought it must be a compliment. In spite of his indifference toward sports, he was pleased to think that the assistant coach had singled him out for special attention.

In a way, this was a laugh. He had been such a miserable flop on the basketball floor, he didn't think anyone would ever want him on any kind of a team.

It made him feel good to think that Mr. McKenzie thought he had what it took to play football.

If he could make the team, it just might be fun to go out.

"To tell you the truth, I never have given much thought to sports. I didn't figure I'd have much of a chance against the real hotshots."

"On the contrary, I think you would do very well. After all, your brother has a lot of natural ability. You should have some too."

Twin spots of crimson stained Del's cheeks. So that was the reason McKenzie had wanted him out for football. He wasn't asking him because he had seen any natural ability in him. Or, that was the way it looked. He just figured that if Doug was good at sports, Del ought to be good too. Well he wasn't buying that.

He might have known there would be some catch to it. It couldn't be anything that he had done on his own. Stiffly he got to his feet.

"I—I'll think about it," he said coldly.

"Don't think about it too long." Coach McKenzie's eyes slitted. "If you're going to try out for the team, you'd better get with it. The fellows have already been practicing for a week. They've got a head start on you. If you want to earn a starting post, you're going to have to get busy, and fast."

Fuming, Del went back to his desk in study hall. If Mr. McKenzie thought that was going to persuade

Football Tryouts

him to go out for football, he'd have to think again. He'd been in Doug's shadow as long as he was going to be. He wasn't going to be there in football too.

Doug, who had been waiting for him, leaned across the aisle and whispered hoarsely. "Did you get to see the coach?"

He nodded. He should have known that Doug would be waiting to find out what had happened, but he wasn't going to tell him—at least not unless he asked. Doug didn't want him on the team so they could play together. He wanted him to try out for football so he could show him up again, the same way he had when they both were out for basketball. Well, Del told himself with growing determination, he wasn't going to let it happen again if he could help it.

"What'd he say?"

No answer. Del found sudden interest in his English book, pretending not to hear.

"What'd he say?"

"He wanted me to go out for the team, but I told him I didn't know whether I could be bothered playing football or not."

Doug's disappointment was keen. "You mean you're not going to try out for the squad?"

"That's right."

"Even after the coach asked you?" As far as Doug was concerned an attitude like that was incredulous.

Del laughed. "I figured one hero in the family is enough."

Doug's lips curled and anger blazed in his eyes. "I didn't know you could be so stupid!"

"Lay off, will you?" Del snarled. "That's all I ask. Lay off!"

2

Sandy's Problem

WHEN DEEDEE and her brothers got back to Fairview after spending the summer at Angle Inlet she could scarcely wait to get to a phone to call Sandy Cole. It seemed as though it had been years since she had seen her best friend. When they were in the car and headed home from the airport she staked out her claim for the telephone ahead of anyone else.

"I get to use it first!"

A thin smile slyly tickled the corners of Doug's mouth. "Why are you so anxious to get to a telephone? Are you going to call Wally Crowder?"

Her cheeks flamed, but she did not reply. She knew Doug and Del when they got started. Nothing could stop them as long as they thought she was getting disgusted about their teasing.

"He's probably got another girl by this time. After all, you can't expect anything else. You've been gone all summer."

She frowned at him. "For your information," she said icily, "I'm going to call Sandy Cole."

Doug groaned. "That's just as bad."

"You're just saying that because you don't want the rest of us to know that you really and truly like her."

"Like her?" he exploded. "Me, like a creep like Sandy Cole? Are you out of your mind?"

She straightened indignantly. "I don't like to have you talk that way. She happens to be my very best friend and I don't like it when people say things like that about her. And I especially don't like it when my brothers talk that way!"

He squirmed. He really didn't mean to talk that way about Sandy. She was nice enough, he guessed —for a girl. If she would only leave him alone, she wouldn't be so bad.

That was all he asked. For her to leave him alone. She ought to know by this time that he didn't want to have anything to do with her. If she started after him again this year he—he didn't know what he'd do, but he'd do something.

Someone changed the subject just then and Doug sighed gratefully. If they kept on, it wouldn't be long until Del would get into the act, needling him about her, and he couldn't take that.

As soon as they got to the Orlis home DeeDee raced for the phone and dialed her friend's number. Sandy answered.

Sandy's Problem   19

"Hello." There was a strange woodenness in her usually gay voice, a hollow, lifeless tone that surely reflected the way Sandy felt.

DeeDee was so excited talking with her friend once more that at first she didn't notice the change in her manner.

"It's me. DeeDee."

"I know—" She sounded as though she didn't particularly care whether she talked with DeeDee or not.

DeeDee asked her about the things she had been doing all summer and how the rest of the kids in their gang were. Sandy mentioned Wally Crowder's parties as the highlights of the summer, and the picnic they had had the week before.

"It must have been a lot of fun." A certain wistfulness crept into DeeDee's voice. "I wish I could have been here."

"It was all right, I guess."

"You must not have had any fun."

"Oh, I did. I had a great time and so did everybody else. It was the best picnic I've ever gone on. A real blast!"

In spite of Sandy's protests, DeeDee had the uneasy feeling that there was something wrong. "Is everything all right, Sandy?"

Silence reigned on the other end of the line. Dee-Dee repeated the question.

"Of course everything's all right!" She spoke

quickly, a bit too quickly, it seemed to her friend, as though she was trying to convince herself and Dee-Dee that she didn't have any problems. "I had a ball all summer." Desperation crept into her voice. "You should have been here. I don't think I've *ever* had so much fun."

Breathlessly Sandy described another party that had been held recently, telling most of the funny things that had happened in minute detail. She told how Wally had invited the kids, making the girls ask the boys and go and get them and everything. She told who had invited who and that Wally had asked if DeeDee was going to be home in time for it.

"He told me that if he knew for sure that you were going to be home within a couple of days or so, he would have waited until you were back to give the party. That's how much he thinks of you."

DeeDee started to reply, but saw that Del was sitting nearby listening to everything she was saying. If she so much as mentioned Wally Crowder's name, she would never hear the end of it.

"That's nice," she said.

"He still thinks you're the cutest girl in school and the one he really wants to go with. He told me that himself, just the other day."

With difficulty DeeDee suppressed a smile. It was good to know that Wally liked her and enjoyed being with her. She liked him too.

Sandy's Problem 21

When she hung up she was vaguely disturbed by Sandy's lack of friendliness. She had thought her friend would come over to see her as soon as she learned that DeeDee was back. Or she expected her friend to invite her to her home, perhaps even to stay all night. They had so many things to talk over, so many things to catch up on.

But she didn't. Actually, Sandy sounded as though she didn't want DeeDee to come around at all. She sounded very distant, almost strange. Maybe Sandy didn't want to be her best friend anymore. The thought chilled her.

When she went to school that first day of the new term DeeDee lingered in the corridor just inside the front door, waiting uneasily for Sandy to come in. She had decided that there was something wrong with Sandy. Her friend hadn't even sounded like herself on the phone. After Sandy acted as though she didn't care to see her, DeeDee had scarcely been able to sleep that night.

Maybe Sandy had a new friend, she reasoned, or for some reason had decided that she didn't want to be around her very much this school year. Maybe this was her way of letting her know that she didn't want her as a best friend. DeeDee moved about uneasily, watching for Sandy's familiar figure on the walk outside.

By this time the kids were streaming into the school. Most of them called out to DeeDee as they hurried past. She spoke mechanically to those she knew. She didn't know what she would do if Sandy didn't want to be her friend anymore. There wasn't anybody else in Fairview that she even cared about. If Sandy wouldn't be her friend anymore she—she—

A familiar car pulled to a stop at the curb and a slight figure got out.

Sandy! DeeDee felt the breath squeeze out of her lungs. She couldn't just stand there. She—

Sandy rushed breathlessly up the steps and flung open the door. She stopped suddenly as she saw her friend, tears suddenly clouding her eyes.

"DeeDee!" Her voice broke. "DeeDee!"

Numbly the other girl stared. "Sandy!"

Her friend came over to her, lips trembling uncertainly. This time there was no mistaking it. There was something wrong. There had to be!

"What's the matter?" DeeDee asked, speaking softly so on one else could possibly hear. "Has something happened?"

"Oh, I'm so glad that you're home!" Her voice broke. "I've got to talk to somebody and there's no one else who would understand."

"What is it?"

She grasped DeeDee's arm and squeezed it convulsively. "I can't tell you here, but it—it's been awful; I've never gone through such a terrible summer in my whole life!"

Sandy's Problem

Together they turned and made their way down the corridor to their homeroom. DeeDee ached for her friend, but in spite of that, relief surged over her. Regardless of what had taken place, Sandy was still her friend. That was all that mattered to her at the moment.

At noon Sandy waited for her the way she had done the year before, and they went to the cafeteria together for lunch. DeeDee had already guessed the source of the trouble that was disturbing her friend. She had hinted at it in her letters during the summer and Wally Crowder had mentioned something about her folks one of the few times he wrote to her. With all of that, however, DeeDee still hadn't expected her friend to say anything about it in school that noon where there was a chance that they might be overheard. She was surprised when Sandy started to tell her what had happened as soon as they sat down.

"It's been terrible!" she exclaimed, her voice little more than a whisper. "Daddy's been—been drunk most of the time and—and he and Mother have been fighting something awful! I don't know what's going to happen."

Impulsively DeeDee reached out her hand and squeezed Sandy's fingers. "Oh, I'm so sorry."

Sandy's throat constricted convulsively until she could not go on. She stopped and swallowed hard.

DeeDee waited silently until her friend was able to continue.

"For a while I thought that everything was going to be all right. We all did. Daddy said that he was going to quit drinking and gambling and running around and was even going to start going to church—"

DeeDee nodded seriously. She knew that if Danny were talking to Mr. Cole, he would tell him that God was the only answer to his problems. Maybe someone had been talking to him about his need of the Lord Jesus Christ.

"If he's thinking that way, chances are he'll get straightened out sooner or later."

But Sandy shook her head. "He did go to church two or three times to please Mother and me, and for a couple of weeks I guess he didn't drink. At least we didn't know about it if he did. But it wasn't long until he said that going to church was for the birds. He quit going and it wasn't long until he was drinking again." Desperation gleamed in her eyes. "It's no use, DeeDee! He's completely hopeless. He'll *never* stop drinking and be what he ought to be!"

DeeDee gazed at her friend. She had never felt so helpless in her life. If there was only something she could say that would give Sandy hope and encouragement. If there was only some way that she could be of help to her! But there wasn't. She couldn't do a thing.

Sandy's Problem   25

"I—I'll be praying for you," she said lamely.

Sandy only stared at her. That was no consolation to her. She had never known what prayer was or how it could really help. "I—I haven't even told you the worst of it!" she continued.

"You—you haven't?" That seemed incredible to DeeDee. How could things possibly be any worse than what Sandy had described?

"Daddy and Mother have been fighting so much that he got mad a couple of nights ago and said that he couldn't stand living with her anymore. He said she nagged at him all the time, and he didn't have to put up with it anymore. So he moved out and said that he was—he was—" She paused, her lips trembling. "He said that he's going to get a divorce!"

DeeDee gasped. She knew that a lot of people got divorces, but the word was still frightening to her. And she knew it was to Sandy too.

"You don't think he will, do you?"

"I don't know. He was awfully angry and drunk when he said it. But that's only part of the trouble. Now he's got Mother so mad that she says if he doesn't get a divorce, she is going to. She says he's been drinking so much that his business is going to pieces and it won't be long until he doesn't have anything. So, she's threatening to divorce him and get what she can now, before it's too late!"

DeeDee mumbled something or other—softly, so

nobody would hear. It didn't sound as though anything or anyone would be able to help the Cole family! And especially Sandy. It was no wonder she was so bewildered and upset.

3

Ballcarrier Del

DEL STILL HADN'T made up his mind to go out for football when school was out the first day. In a way he wanted to, but in another way he didn't feel that he could risk going out and having Doug make a fool of him again. He was feeling out of sorts and very sorry for himself when he got off the bus and walked down the lane to the Orlis home.

It was almost 6:30 that night when Doug got home. Del had already done the chores and the family was waiting to eat.

"Hi." Doug's grin was broad. He'd had a good practice and it looked as though he had a chance to make the team.

Del looked up. "It's about time you got here," he grumbled.

"What's the matter with you?" Doug slipped out of his jacket and started for his room. "You act as though you've swallowed a rusty nail."

Del grimaced. "There's nothing wrong with me. I'm just fed up with having to do all the work around here, that's all."

"What do you mean, you have to do all the work? I told you to let the chores go until I got home from football practice and I'd help you do them."

He stood belligerently. "Sure, you'll help me when you get home!" he mimicked. "But who wants to stumble around doing chores in the dark? Answer me that."

"You could go out for football too, you know." There was a thin edge to his voice. "Then we could both work together and you wouldn't be complaining about having to do everything around here."

A sneer tugged at the corner of Del's mouth. "Who wants to go out for football?"

"If you weren't afraid of getting bumped a little, you'd be out for football the way the other guys are. You could be helping the team."

The other boy's eyes blazed. "I'll show you whether I'm afraid to go out for football or not!"

"You wouldn't dare!"

Del pulled in a shallow breath. "Just you wait until tomorrow! I'll show you whether or not I dare to go out for football! You can't call me a coward and get away with it!"

"I'll believe it when I see it."

"You'll see it! I'm promising you that much right now!"

Ballcarrier Del

The following afternoon Del went down to the locker room after class and reported to Alex Smith.

"I'm glad you decided to come out for the team, Del. I've been hearing some good things about you."

He scowled but did not reply.

Doug was visibly surprised and said so. "So you finally decided to come out."

Del frowned. "I get ribbed for not playing football and now I get it for coming out. What gives?"

"Nothing. I'm just surprised to see you here, that's all. I thought you'd be home playing with that stupid crow of yours."

Mr. McKenzie came up just then with the team manager. "Joe'll issue you your equipment," he told Del. "When you're dressed, report to Coach Smith on the field."

Del nodded grimly. He still didn't think much of the idea of trying out for the team, but he wasn't going to have that brother of his spouting off about him anymore. Doug would find out soon enough whether he was afraid to take a few hard knocks.

Doug stopped beside him momentarily before going out on the field. "I'm sure glad you came out, Del."

He looked up, a surly curl to his lips. "Knock it off, will you?"

"You'll find out that it's the greatest sport there is. After you've been out for a couple of weeks, you'll really dig it!"

Del shrugged. He didn't know what was the matter with that brother of his or why he thought everyone had to be so up-tight over football just because he liked it. As far as Del was concerned, it just wasn't his bag. He wouldn't be out for the squad now if he didn't have to prove something to Doug. And as soon as he'd proved it he was going to split. He wasn't going to knock himself out for any stupid game.

On the field Alex Smith called the squad to order.

"It's getting close to the time when we play our first game," he began. "I hope you fellows are all looking forward to it as much as I am."

Several of them grinned.

"We're going to be working hard. Harder than you've ever worked in your life before. We're going to work on fundamentals until you all know how to block and tackle and pass and kick. If you're afraid of working, or if you're afraid of getting knocked around, now's the time to turn in your suit. . . ."

Del glanced angrily at his brother as the coach continued to talk. It sounded as though Doug had been spouting off to the new coach about him. He must have told Alex that Del hadn't come out for football because he was soft and afraid of getting hit.

"But, if you stay with me and do what you're told—" Alex was saying, "if you put out for me every minute, you'll earn your chance to play, and

Ballcarrier Del

Fairview will have the finest football team we've ever had. And there've been some good ones in the past. Believe me...."

When Alex had finished talking, he led them out to the practice field and set them to work. Del glanced at his brother. "If this is what football practice is like, you can have it. It's for the birds!"

"I knew you couldn't take it."

Del colored. "Who can't take it? You watch me. I'll show you whether I can take it or not."

That was the trouble with that conceited brother of his, he stormed inwardly. Everything had to go his way. The things he liked to do were all right. The things Del liked didn't amount to anything. He had to be the wheel—the guy everybody looked up to and talked about.

He acted as though he wanted Del to be out for football, but Del knew the real reason for that. He didn't care what anybody else had to say about it. Well, he'd show Doug whether he was afraid to play football or not. He'd probably make a mess of everything though, and get kicked off the squad at the first cut. But even that wouldn't matter. All he cared about was proving that pig-headed brother of his didn't know what he was talking about when he said that Del was afraid.

The first few days he was just one of the fellows, lost in the numbers of the big, uncut squad. He jogged around the track the prescribed number of times and practiced tackling and blocking with the others. Doug watched him curiously.

"How do you like it?"

"It's all right, I guess." Actually, he still felt that he could get along very well without football. It was all right to goof around with if he didn't have anything else to do, but it wasn't his idea of the way to spend an exciting fall afternoon or night.

Doug continued to talk, keeping his voice down so no one else would hear what he had to say. "I overheard Alex and McKenzie talking about you this afternoon."

Del scowled. "I suppose I'm going to be the first guy to get the boot when they cut the squad."

"It didn't sound that way. They talked as though they've been watching you closely. McKenzie thinks you've got the speed it takes to make a good ball-carrier, and you know that he coaches the backs."

Del eyed him with a degree of suspicion. "Just who're you trying to kid?"

"I'm giving you the straight goods. From what I heard, I wouldn't be surprised if they try you at halfback, or maybe at end."

Del went on into the locker room and began to undress to shower, without saying anything more. There was undoubtedly some catch to what Doug just told him. There had to be. They could only be building him up for a letdown. They'd pull the rug out from under him, and Doug and the others would

Ballcarrier Del

laugh when he fell on his face. But, he'd fool them. It didn't matter that much to him. He'd already proved his point to Doug. That was all that really mattered.

Actually, he only half believed Doug when he told him that the coaches were considering him for halfback or end. It wasn't that he thought Doug was lying to him. He had never known his brother to do that and didn't think he would start now. But he figured maybe Doug had only heard half of what Alex Smith and McKenzie had said, and tried to guess at the rest.

After all, he'd never been out for football before. They couldn't be serious about making him a ballcarrier. That had to be a goof-up of some kind. But, he was surprised the next afternoon when McKenzie gave him the chance to play in the backfield with the second string during scrimmage.

"This is only a scrimmage session," Alex said, looking over the players critically, "but I want you to give us everything you've got. Just remember that it won't be long until we'll start making cuts in the size of the squad. The fellows who are going to make it with us are the ones who try a little harder, the ones who scrap for that last half a yard."

Del winced. He knew what that meant. He would be off the squad for good. He tried to tell himself that it really didn't matter to him, but he found that it did. He *wanted* to make it.

They had been playing for several minutes when he first carried the ball. He took it on a quick hand-off from the quarterback, hesitated for his blockers to get into position, and knifed forward. The hole in the line opened and closed, but not in time to stop him. He wriggled through, feinting and sidestepping his way past the linebacker, and drove for a ten-yard gain.

Doug, who was playing with the first string, grinned as he moved back into position. Del, who was eyeing him curiously, saw the grin and wondered about it. It wasn't like Doug to care whether he accomplished anything or not.

The quarterback called the same play again, but this time the first string was set for it. Still, they were able to stop Del only after he had picked up another six yards. They drove him to the ground with a bone-jarring tackle. That didn't bother him at all. In fact, he enjoyed the body contact.

The coach blew his whistle.

"Nice going, Davis," Alex exclaimed. "That was real good. You've got the drive I like to see. I had a hunch that you were going to do OK."

Doug's grin broadened and he nodded approvingly.

"I want you to suit up with the first string tomorrow."

Del mumbled something under his breath in response to the expressions of approval from the other

Ballcarrier Del

fellows. He was glad to hear what they thought of him and all of that, but what really mattered to him was Doug's attitude.

He couldn't say that he didn't like what he had experienced playing football. There was something exhilarating about hitting the line with all the power in his lithe young body. It was fun to carry the ball and to make a good, clean tackle. But he still wasn't sure that winning a game meant a great deal to him. At least it didn't mean as much to him as it did to Doug. It never had. Neither did getting a starting assignment mean that he'd reached the top of the mountain.

He didn't think to say anything to Danny about what had happened at practice when he and Doug got home that evening. It was his brother who had to tell the family about it.

"Now, that *is* good news," Danny said. "I was sure that McKenzie had seen something in you that made him think you'd make a good player or he'd never have encouraged you to go out for the team."

DeeDee spoke up. "We've watched some of the practices, and Sandy thinks you're going to be on the first string for sure, Del. She says that she just *loves* to watch you run."

Doug snickered.

His brother turned to him. "What's the matter with you?" he demanded.

"You'll find out." He laughed again. "I'm not going to say a thing; you'll find out soon enough."

Del pulled in a long breath. So Doug thought Sandy Cole was going to try to get her claws into him! Well, he'd show her! He'd show everyone!

"I'm warning you, DeeDee!" He spoke darkly. "I'm warning you!"

"About what?"

"You know what."

Her eyes danced. "And what makes you think that I know what you're talking about? I haven't done or said anything to get you so worked up."

The corners of his mouth twitched. "And you'd better not, if you know what's good for you."

Doug laughed again. "I can tell you one thing about Sandy, Del. She's real friendly. You'll find her easy to get acquainted with."

Del frowned. "You lay off too."

"I won't do a thing." Doug snickered. "Knowing Sandy, I won't have to."

4

Jealousy

ON THE PRACTICE FIELD Del continued to show progress. He wasn't as adept at handling the ball as Doug and Larry Larson were, and he didn't know much about blocking and tackling, but he more than made up for his deficiencies in the fundamentals department with his shifty, broken-field running. He seemed to have an inborn sense of timing and deceptiveness that was bewildering to the defense. He was quick and agile in the backfield, able to explode through a hole in the line that was a sliver wide and opened only for a fraction of a heartbeat.

In the first scrimmage as a member of the first string he followed his interference up to the line of scrimmage, cut sharply to the left as a blocker was taken out, and knifed between tackle and guard for a thirty-eight-yard touchdown run.

Alex Smith grinned his approval as the teams lined up for the kickoff.

"What did I tell you about that Davis kid?" McKenzie asked. "He's a natural broken-field runner, isn't he?"

"He's still rough on fundamentals, but he's got a lot of style," Alex acknowledged. "I think we're going to see a lot of him before the season is over."

"You can say that again. I'm going to work hard on him."

There was only one thing about Del that bothered Alex. He seemed a bit too casual about the game. Alex liked players who had such a fierce desire to win that they cried when they were beaten. Guys who would get out on the field and scrap through every second of the game, whether they were fifty points ahead or that many behind. He wasn't sure that Del really cared that much about football. At the moment, that was a big question mark.

In the locker room when the practice session was over, a couple of regulars came over to where Doug was dressing.

"Man, did you see that run your brother made?" Larry Larson asked. "He looked great."

Doug's cheeks colored. "He got a lucky break and a couple of good blocks, that's all."

But Larry did not agree with him. "That wasn't luck, I can tell you that much. He outfoxed the second team, that's what happened. I don't think I ever saw a high school run like that."

Doug muttered something to his friend and turned

Jealousy 39

away. Something inside him made him fume. It was one thing having Del out for football. He liked that. And he was glad that the fellows thought he was good. But to have them act as though he was the greatest guy to ever put on a pair of football shoes was something else again.

"He can't tackle and he can't block. Don't forget that."

"Just the same, I'm glad he's playing for us instead of against us. He's going to score his share of TD's before the season's over."

Doug and Del went home together that evening after football practice was over, but for some reason the air was strained between them. They walked almost half a mile in the warm September air before either of them said a word.

"You know, Doug, I'm beginning to find out that you were right about football." Del could not contain his grin. "It's a lot of fun."

Doug glared at him. "Maybe you think that now, but it's not such a breeze when the guys on defense have had a chance to sharpen their tackling. Wait until October. When they smear you then, you'll know that you've been hit. And that's the truth."

Del shrugged his unconcern. "Maybe it is, but if they can't catch you, they can't tackle you."

Doug flinched. He hadn't expected his brother to get so conceited in such a hurry. "Big deal! You've been out for football a week or so and you're already talking like an all-American just because you've had a couple of lucky runs."

"The coach seems to think I'm doing all right."

Doug's resentment built. Del would soon learn that playing football wasn't only running with the ball. There were ten other players out on the field helping him. If some of the other guys missed their assignments a few times he'd soon find out what a great ballcarrier he was. They'd knock that silly smile off his mug in a big hurry.

That's what they ought to do, he thought. *Let a couple of big tacklers sift through and nail him once or twice. That would take a lot of the conceit out of him.*

When they were near home Del turned to Doug.

"I'm going out to see Barney for a while Saturday morning. Want to go along?"

Bitterness curled Doug's lips. "And why would I want to go out and see Barney?"

"You ought to do some of the things that I like to do," Del reminded him. "After all, I went out for football because you kept begging me to."

Doug snorted. "Big deal!'

On Friday evening the Fairview eleven met Foreston. Both Del and Doug were in the starting lineup and got to play most of the game, but it was obvious from the first play that Del was easily the star. Aside from a couple of glaring errors that stemmed from his lack of experience, he played a superb game.

Jealousy

Three times in the first half he carried the ball for long yardage. Almost single-handedly he set up Fairview's first touchdown midway in the opening quarter. On the third play of the second quarter he took a hand-off from the quarterback, followed Doug over tackle, and exploded into the open for what would have been an easy touchdown had the ball not squirted from his hands.

A groan of dismay went up from the crowd who had come out to see the game. Del's cheeks flushed and his anger at himself churned within. Doug grinned impishly.

"That was a great play, 'all-American.' Did you hear the crowd cheering?"

The corners of his mouth tightened. "Lay off, will you?"

Nevertheless, Fairview won the first game and Del had much to do with it.

He continued to sparkle on the football field, solidifying his hold on his backfield post with the varsity. In the second game he showed the coaching staff that they had not made a mistake in using him.

On Fairview's first offensive play of the game the quarterback gave Del the ball. He dropped back quickly, as though to pass, faked a handoff to the fullback who came charging past him, and darted through a hole off tackle. A groan went up from the crowd as two tacklers converged upon him. He seemed to hesitate indecisively before flicking past both tacklers and scooting into the flat. When the safety finally came up to drop him, he had made a first in ten with two yards to spare. The men in the stands were looking at one another in bewilderment, asking who had been carrying the ball.

"It's one of the Davis kids," someone said.

"I don't know who he is, but I can tell you one thing right now. That kid's going to be great when he get a little more experience."

DeeDee, who was sitting just in front of them, beamed. She hadn't thought she would ever be proud of Del. Not that way, at least. But she was. Especially when Sandy turned to her.

"It must be cool having two brothers who can play ball the way Doug and Del do."

She smiled. They both gave her such a bad time they seemed to be the biggest pests in town, but she was proud of them both. She was glad that Del was out for football instead of fooling around with Blackie or Jumper or one of his other pets. At least the rest of the kids at school wouldn't think he was such an oddball.

Del carried the ball on the next play for another six yards and a cheer went up from the stands. She added her voice to the swell of acclamation.

That look gleamed in Sandy's eyes again, the same look DeeDee had seen when Doug distinguished himself on the basketball court.

Jealousy

"Oh, DeeDee, you've got the *cutest* brothers!"

DeeDee groaned inwardly. The joy went out of the game for her. It wouldn't be so bad if Del and Doug weren't so stupid when it came to Sandy. In fact, it would be very nice if one or the other would see what a cute girl she was and would show just a little interest in her. But no, they couldn't do that. They had to act as though Sandy was poison or something. Even if they were her brothers, they made her sick.

The game wasn't as one-sided as Del's initial success made it appear. Paxton came clawing back in the second quarter to drive one touchdown across and threaten with a second in the dying moments of the half. A long pass midway in the third quarter put Fairview ahead, and another touchdown near the end of the game on successive runs by the new, fleet-footed back, gave them a twelve-point lead.

In the locker room at the close of the game Alex Smith was jubilant.

"You fellows played a good game tonight," he began, looking around at his team. "And I mean all of you. I was proud of every one of you. You looked more like a major college outfit than a high school team."

The fellows beamed. It always meant more when the coach was satisfied with the way they played.

"And Davis," Alex continued, turning toward Del, "you played a great game. If you keep this up, you're going to be an important man in our offense."

One of the tackles leaned over to Doug and whispered hoarsely. "I thought you were the great football hero of the Davis triplets, but it looks now as though you've been deposed."

Del couldn't help overhearing the remark. He squirmed uncomfortably. It made him feel funny to have the guys talk that way about him, and he didn't know for sure why. Not that it wasn't good to give Doug a little of his own medicine. Now maybe he'd find out what it was like to have everyone talk about Del instead of him. He'd know what Del had gone through when Doug was such a star on the basketball court. He glanced at his brother, who flushed quickly and turned away.

At home that evening Doug was strangely quiet. Del tried to talk with him, but he would only answer a direct question. Finally his brother could stand it no longer.

"That was a good game, wasn't it?"

Doug scowled but did not look up. "It was all right, I guess," he muttered. Little of his old enthusiasm was left in his voice.

Del noticed Doug's reluctance to talk about the game with a certain grim satisfaction. He knew exactly how Doug felt. And, for the moment, at least, he was glad for it. Doug had made him feel the same way often enough.

"You were right about one thing," Del went on,

Jealousy

"I do like to play football a lot better than I ever thought that I would. His dark eyes narrowed as he gauged Doug's reaction.

His brother flinched.

"It wasn't such a big deal," Doug murmured. "You happened to get lucky in one game, that's all."

"I didn't do so bad last week either, if you'll remember."

"So you were lucky in two games."

Del's gaze met his. "That's not what Coach Smith said. To tell you the truth, Doug, he thinks that I'm pretty good."

Doug snorted. "There you go! Don't break your arm trying to pat yourself on the back. The season's just starting, you know. You've still got plenty of time to flub things up."

Del laughed. He knew that he shouldn't have, but he couldn't resist the temptation to needle his brother. "And just exactly what's the matter with you?" he demanded. "Can't you stand to have anyone else get a little glory?"

Doug glared at him and pushed the chair back so violently as he got to his feet that he knocked it over. "You're some guy!" he exploded. "You won't go out for football until I practically get down on my knees and beg you to. Then when you do play OK in a couple of games you get the idea that you're a real star. Big deal!"

"What's the matter? Are you jealous?"

"Jealous?" Doug's eyes glazed. "Me jealous of you? You make me sick!"

Del stared at him.

There was no doubt about it. He had gotten it back on Doug, but good. He ought to feel great. But he didn't. Actually, he didn't feel good at all. It made him feel cheap and unclean. He wanted to apologize to his brother, but right then he couldn't. Doug wouldn't listen.

The next morning when they got up, Doug spoke to him, but there was a barrier between them. Things weren't the way they had been before. It bothered both of them.

5

Drunken Quarrel

When Sandy got home from the football game that evening she saw that her dad's car was in the driveway. A wave of relief engulfed her. That meant that he was at home and the chances were that he wasn't drinking, at least that night. She had reached the place where she was thankful if he was sober for even one day. He hadn't been at home or sober very much in the past few months.

But as she stepped into the living room the strength left her body and her stomach knotted painfully. At first glance she saw that something was wrong—terribly wrong.

Her dad was home all right. He was sitting in a straight-backed chair staring at their color television set. His face was bloated and unnaturally flushed. The whites of his eyes were veined with red and there was a belligerent set to his jaw.

Her mother had been crying, Sandy saw. But for

the moment at least the tears were dried on her cheeks and her face was hard as stone.

Sandy looked from one to the other helplessly, and tried to speak with a gaiety she certainly did not feel. "Hi." She searched their faces hopefully—anxious for some small sign that all was well between them. But there was no evidence that they were in harmony about anything.

"Hello, Sandy." Her dad's voice was solemn and slow of syllable. It was only with great self-control that he was able to keep the words from slurring together. Sandy noticed that too. She had long since become adept at reading the little signs that would indicate whether her dad was drinking. As she saw that he had been drinking heavily, something died within her.

She was still staring at him when her mother spoke. "I don't know how you can have the gall to even speak to your daughter when you're in *that* condition." Venom poisoned the words.

Mr. Cole jerked erect, belligerence and arrogance overriding the self-pity he was experiencing at the moment.

"I told you that I'd leave," he stammered, stumbling over the words. "Anytime you don't want me around here, I can leave. I don't stay anyplace where I'm not wanted." He was talking to his wife, but as he spoke he stared fixedly at Sandy, who had stopped just inside the door. "Nobody has to tell

Drunken Quarrel 49

me to leave more than once. No one cares anything about me around here, anyway. I'd just as well go someplace where—where I'm appreciated."

Mrs. Cole's anxiety and shame and self-pity spilled over in a savage blast of hate.

"That's right!" she cried. "Nobody around here cares anything about you. And do you want to know why?"

His lips were trembling, but for the moment he could not speak.

"Nobody here cares anything about you because you've killed any love that we've ever had for you! It's your own fault!"

Sandy eyed her helplessly. She knew exactly how her mother felt. She felt the same way when she saw her dad in the condition he was in. Sometimes it made her so mad that she felt she never wanted to see him again.

Only, deep within, she knew that wasn't true. She got so angry with him because she loved him so very much and hated to see him in a drunken stupor. At the moment she ached so deeply inside that she didn't think she could stand it.

"If that's the way you feel about me I'd just as well be dead!" Tears trembled on her dad's eyelids.

Sandy had never known him to cry when he was sober, except when Grandmother died and he stood with her and Mother beside the grave after the funeral service. But when he was drunk, tears were a common thing. They didn't mean anything at all.

"Oh, Daddy!" she cried, the words tearing from her lips. She couldn't help it! No matter what he had done, he was her dad and she couldn't bear to have him talk that way.

But it seemed to have no effect on her mother.

"That's right," she blurted angrily, "try to get us all to feel sorry for you because you're so abused by everybody. Well, I'm going to tell you right now that it's not going to work this time. Neither Sandy nor I care where you go or what happens to you! You've hurt us so much that we're past caring!"

Sandy jerked about to face her mother. That wasn't true! She did care about her dad and what happened to him. That was why she felt so bad when she saw that he had been drinking again. And her mother cared too. Only the hurt she experienced was so great that she couldn't control her tongue.

Suddenly Sandy could stand it no longer. Bursting into tears, she whirled and dashed upstairs.

"Now you've got her crying too!" Mrs. Cole's voice drifted up to Sandy. "Are you satisfied?"

That night Sandy lay on her bed in the darkness, sobbing into her pillow. Time ceased to exist. She was suspended in some miserable, bottomless shaft from which there was no escaping. A paralyzing numbness took hold of her. She could feel, but for the moment she was completely powerless to act.

She hadn't realized that she had not closed the

Drunken Quarrel 51

door to her bedroom until her parents' angry voices drifted up to her. She heard some of the terrible things they were saying to each other—things she would have stopped herself from hearing if she could—awful things that she was sure neither of them meant. She knew they only said them in an angered effort to hurt each other.

Her dad raged at her mother for nagging at him incessantly and trying to turn Sandy against him. Then she heard him use profanity, as though trying to shock the hysterical woman he had married into silence. Sandy's mother called him a no-good drunken gambler and wondered aloud why she had ever married him.

When anger and cursing didn't back her down, Mr. Cole switched to his more familiar position of self-pity. The switch came suddenly and heavy with tears.

"If that's the way you feel about me, you aren't going to have to put up with me anymore. I'll leave. That's what I'll do. I'll leave!" His drunken voice was thick and slurred. "There are plenty of places I can stay where people will be nice to me. I don't have to stick around here and have you yell at me as though I'm—I'm your slave! I'll up and leave. Then maybe you'll be sorry for the way you've treated me."

Sandy heard him stagger noisily to his feet. She sat up, listening. It wasn't the first time he had threatened to leave them. It seemed that every time he and Mother had an argument the last few weeks, he had threatened to pack up and move. She had begun to believe that it was all a bluff, that he talked a lot about it but it was something that he would never do.

"I'm not going to stay where I'm not wanted," he repeated. "I can tell you that right now. If you aren't going to be nice to me, I'll just pack my things and go!"

Mrs. Cole's voice rose to a shout.

"I wish you would! I wish that you'd go so far away that Sandy and I would never see or hear from you again!"

That seemed to stop him. He must have slumped into a chair and closed his eyes the way Sandy had seen him do so often when he was in that condition. At last he spoke again.

"You think I'm bluffing, don't you? You think that I won't do it!"

"I couldn't care less! And if you want the truth, I hope you do leave! It'll be better for all three of us!"

There was a long painful silence.

When they resumed talking their voices lowered until Sandy could not hear what they were saying. If they followed the usual pattern, they would probably make up now. They usually did after an argument like this. And, if that was what happened,

Drunken Quarrel

Dad would probably stay sober for a week or so—just long enough so she would think that *this* time he really meant it. *This* time things were going to be completely different.

But they wouldn't be. She knew that now. They would never be any different. He would keep right on drinking as long as he lived. He didn't seem to be able to help himself—or so it seemed to the distraught young girl.

She couldn't really blame her mother for getting mad at him because of the way he acted. Sandy got mad too. And there were times when she said things to him that she was sorry for later. But she didn't like it when her mother talked so terribly to him. She read the hurt in his eyes and knew how horrible he must feel. But, then, she knew how bad her mother felt too. And she knew how many nights she cried herself to sleep. It wasn't easy for her, either, having Daddy the way he was.

Why couldn't her dad and mother be like other kids' parents? she wondered. Why couldn't they be like Danny and Kay Orlis? Danny and Kay weren't the Davis triplets' folks at all, but they didn't fight with each other and really cared what DeeDee and the boys did. That was the reason they had set up rules for them.

But it didn't matter to her folks, she thought, where she went or who she was with or what she did. They didn't care anything about her and weren't concerned about raising her to be the sort of person they could be proud of. All they ever thought about was themselves.

Sandy didn't realize how long she had lain on her bed in the darkness, but at last she heard her mother come quietly up the stairs and stop at her door. She opened her eyes and waited.

"Sandy." There was a guarded knock. "Sandy."

She did not answer. She couldn't talk to her mother right then. She didn't want to talk to anyone.

"Sandy!"

When there was still no answer, Mrs. Cole went on down the hall to her own bedroom. The girl listened until she heard the metallic click of the lock. That meant Dad was still in the house—probably sprawled on the divan in the living room in a drunken stupor.

Sandy began to sob once more, crying bitterly until at last she fell asleep.

6

Brotherly Feud

DEL WAS EASILY THE STAR of the next football game. He had been learning more about the fundamentals of the game as the weeks went on and he wasn't making the number of mistakes that he had made earlier in the season. He scored a touchdown after a twenty-eight-yard run in the first half to keep Fairview in the game. He got another on a kickoff return seconds before the gun sounded the end of the last quarter, to nose out their opponents 28-26. A rousing cheer went up for him as he left the field.

Doug came up beside him.

"You did all right tonight," he murmured. It was hard for him to say that much, but he felt that he had to make some comment about the way his brother had played.

Del glanced his direction, a smile twisting one corner of his mouth. "Did all right?" He meant his remark to be a joke, but it was barbed when it came out. "I guess I did all right. I was the hero."

Envy and anger mingled in his brother's eyes. "You don't think *much* of yourself, do you?"

"Why not? I know I'm good."

"Oh, brother! I've never seen anyone as high-hat as you are!"

"Who's high-hat? You're just jealous because the crowd didn't cheer for you the way they did for me. That's all that's eating you. You're jealous because you can't play football the way I can."

Doug snorted in indignation. He had been disgusted with Del at other times, but he had never felt the way he did right then.

Jealous of Del? He had never heard anything so ridiculous. And it all came about just because that brother of his got a little lucky at the start of the football season before anyone else was up to peak form.

He'd find out what it was like to hang onto his position a little later, when the other guys got to going good. Then Del would learn that he wasn't anything so super special, after all.

"That's a laugh," he snorted. "That's a big laugh! The guys will all die laughing when they hear about it."

Del's grin was transparent and infuriating to his brother.

"I don't know about that. To tell the truth, I didn't see anybody laughing a little while ago." He drew in a deep breath. "The fact is, I thought they

Brotherly Feud

were impressed. Alex Smith and McKenzie seem to think I could help Fairview have an undefeated season. Now, what do you think of that?"

"I think they must be out of their minds," Doug murmured.

"That's not the way I see it."

Doug sucked in a quick breath. "You make me sick with all that stupid conceit!"

Del stared incredulously at him, his smile fading. Anger rushed in to take its place. "That goes double!" he blurted.

"OK! If that's the way you feel about it! OK! I can get along without you very easy! Don't you forget it!" Doug spun on his heel and left his brother abruptly, intending to go on into the school and down to the locker room alone. He was on the steps of the school building when Larry Larson came up beside him.

"Man! Can Del ever carry that ball!' Admiration filled in his voice.

Doug grunted something unintelligible.

"If Del doesn't get hurt, I think he'll be able to give us a perfect season. There isn't *anybody* he can't score on."

"So I've heard."

"You sure don't act very happy about it. You talked so much about getting him out for football or basketball that I thought you'd be more excited than anyone else over the way he's playing."

"I am," Doug retorted, although the resentful tone in his voice belied his words. "Only I get fed up hearing him tell me how good he is all the time!"

Doug showered and dressed with care, his thoughts churning. It wasn't that he objected to the idea that Del was finally out for football and was beginning to make a name for himself. He had always wanted Del to be as excited about sports as he was. And the team needed a fellow who could run the way Del could.

He would have been thrilled with the way Del was doing, if only his brother wasn't so arrogant and overbearing about it. He was so conceited that Doug didn't see how anyone could stand it. He acted as though nobody in town had ever made a touchdown or a long run. And that stupid, superior little grin of his that always flashed on when he talked about the way he could gain ground or score, was sickening. Doug couldn't help it. He felt like booting Del.

When he finished dressing he went out of the building alone. Usually he didn't like the idea of having to make the long walk out to the farm without company, and he would have waited half an hour or so to walk with Del. On this particular evening, however, he rushed off as quickly as possible. Being alone was better than having to listen to his conceited brother blow about the way he had

Brotherly Feud 59

carried the ball and the long runs he was going to make the rest of the season.

* * *

Alex was happier with his new coaching job than Robin had even known him to be since they had been married. He enjoyed working with the boys and matching wits with the other coaches in the area —and especially when he could win. He had always had the fierce desire for victory that he liked to see in his players.

He enjoyed coaching, but he enjoyed the counseling portion of his job as well. He had majored in psychology at college and now was serving the Fairview school system as guidance counselor. Surprisingly, he talked a great deal about both responsibilities.

"To tell you the truth, I don't know which I enjoy the most, Robin," he said one evening. "On the football field I have some tremendous opportunities. There's no doubt of that. I can teach the kids how to work together and to think for themselves in an emergency. I can teach them fair play and good sportsmanship and all the other traits that make for good citizenship."

She nodded. It seemed strange for her to hear Alex talking about such things. She loved him a great deal, but he had never seemed interested in anyone else before, other than himself, and possibly her and their families. Now he seemed genuinely concerned about the kids he was working with.

"And in counseling I have a chance to help the kids who aren't out for sports to get their hangups straightened out and to become more honest, worthwhile citizens. It gives me the opportunity to help them see that the most important thing in life is to live honorably before their friends and neighbors and to be good American citizens who are concerned about helping each other."

"I know just how you feel."

Alex crossed to the table and poured himself another cup of coffee, still talking about the work he did at the high school.

"I didn't realize what serious problems these kids have until I started working on this job. I tell you, Robin, a lot of parents wouldn't sleep nights if they knew the sort of things that were disturbing their teenagers."

She smiled. "I'm sure of that; but when I think back, I seem to remember that you and I had our share of problems when we were in high school."

"Yeah, and we both should have been kicked for getting married the way we did."

She stiffened suddenly. She felt the same way about their marriage, but, strangely enough, it bothered her more than she would admit to hear Alex say anything about it.

Brotherly Feud

"I'm glad to know how you feel about me." In spite of herself, acid thinly laced her voice.

"Now, Robin, you know I didn't mean it that way. I was thinking about my having to quit school the way I did and all the trouble we had before I got back to high school and went on to the university. If we hadn't been mighty lucky, I'd have stayed out of school and would never have been able to finish my education so I could teach. I don't know what our lives would have been like, but I'm sure they wouldn't be what they are now. That's what I meant by saying that we shouldn't have gotten married so soon."

She went over and slipped her arm about his waist.

"I know what you meant, and I feel the same as you do about it," she told him. "Only I don't like to hear you say anything that sounds as though you're not happy with me. I guess I love you too much to want to hear you say those things."

"Oh, I'm happy with you, all right." He paused and for a brief instant a taunting little smile played with the corners of his mouth. "The only time I'm not is when you get on one of those religious kicks of yours and start trying to convert me. That really makes me up-tight."

He was only joking, but his words were a spear piercing her very heart. She had prayed so hard and for so very long for Alex. It was almost as though

God didn't hear—or care—whether he was saved or not.

But, even as she allowed that thought to creep in, she knew that it wasn't true. God did care about her. He had warned her not to marry Alex. He had even warned her not to go out with him. But she had defied His teaching and had gone her own willful way. As far as she had been concerned, she was going to do what she wanted. It didn't make any difference about God's will for her life. Now, she realized that He might leave her with an unsaved mate as a reminder that she had chosen His second best for her life, and that she should have placed Him first.

Alex spoke once more.

"I try to help the kids who come to me the best I know how, but I don't know what to tell some of them, Robin, or how to guide them. It's not easy to help them get straightened out when some of them have made such messes out of their lives."

* * *

Del continued to make a name for himself on the football field with an ease that surprised everyone. His knack for broken-field running continued to improve with each passing game. He could dart in one direction or the other effortlessly, with a deception that left would-be tacklers grasping air instead of the ballcarrier. With a runner like Del, Alex borrowed some of the plays the university used, simplified

Brotherly Feud 63

them a bit for his more youthful squad, and tried them on an unsuspecting opponent. They worked better than he had dared hope. Del's yardage and touchdowns continued to increase. Wherever football was talked in Fairview, the subject inevitably got around to Del. Even Danny began to hear a great deal about the skill of the Davis boy.

"You were late getting started, Del," he said, "but you sure have been picking up ground fast. Kay and I are both proud of you."

"I've just been lucky, that's all."

Danny wasn't so sure that he agreed with him. "The way I look at it, it's a little more than luck. I was talking with Alex yesterday. Believe me, he's as excited about you as everyone else. He says that he's introduced a whole new series of plays for you."

Doug, who was also at the table, mumbled something unintelligibly. Danny turned to him.

"Excuse me, Doug," he said. "I guess I was talking so fast I didn't hear you."

"Oh, nothin'."

Del glanced impishly at his brother.

"I'm sure glad that Doug talked me into going out for football. I didn't know what I was missing—getting my name and picture in the paper and everything. It's really great."

"Listen to the big hero!" Doug's lips curled about the words, shaping them with bitterness.

Disapproval glinted in Kay's eyes. "That wasn't very nice, Doug," she said mildly.

He shoved back from the table and got noisily to his feet. "Maybe it wasn't, but I'm fed up with hearing everybody talking about what a great football player Del is just because he's gotten lucky this season. Anybody could make a name for himself if he got all the breaks the way Del has!"

He stormed into the bedroom that he shared with his brother and slammed the door.

DeeDee looked after him, curiosity gleaming in her eyes.

"Now, what brought that on?" she asked.

No one answered her.

Del went out to do his chores. When it came right down to it, he had to admit that he didn't care too much about football except for the actual game itself. Some of the guys only lived for the sport—practices and all. It was the only thing they ever thought or talked about. But he wasn't like that. He would much rather be playing with Blackie, trying to teach his pet crow some new words, or sitting in Barney's cabin talking with the old Indian trapper, or trying to induce Jumper to come up and eat sugar out of his hand.

He didn't know why, but winning was another thing that didn't mean too much for him. He supposed he enjoyed winning as much as the average guy did, and he got a bit provoked if somebody

Brotherly Feud

missed an assignment or pulled a boner that cost them a few yards, but he didn't feel like Doug did about that sort of thing. Doug's whole week was ruined if he lost a game. He had seen him mope around the place without talking to anyone just because they had lost a close basketball game. And he had gotten so mad at some of his fellow players that he'd hardly speak to them because they did something stupid.

But not Del. He shrugged it off easily—sometimes he wondered if he didn't put it aside too easily to have the consistent drive to win.

He had to admit that the biggest kick he had gotten out of playing football so far was in being able to needle Doug about it. He'd bet Doug wouldn't be after him to go out for any other sport. He'd probably try to talk him out of going out for basketball and baseball if he could. He didn't think he was going to care to play either sport, but he wasn't going to let Doug know that, for a while, anyway. It was too much fun to see him sweat.

7

Divorce

THE MORNING after the football game Sandy awakened reluctantly, shaking the sleep from her swollen eyes. The numbness in her stomach still lay there, unmelted through the long, torturous night. The sun was shining, but that did nothing to change the desolation that gripped her soul. Others could be happy that morning, but not her. She didn't know whether she would ever be happy again.

She got out of bed and was just getting dressed when her mother knocked on the door. "Sandy, are you awake?"

"Come on in." She steeled herself for what was about to come. She wanted to see her mother, but she wasn't sure that she wanted to hear what she would probably say. She wasn't sure that she wanted to talk with anyone just then.

"I'm so glad you're up," Mrs. Cole said, coming hesitantly into the room. "I—I've got to talk with

Divorce

you, Sandy." Her eyes were dark and strangely sunken. It was obvious that she, too, had been crying most of the night.

"Is Daddy still here?" Sandy wanted to know.

Her mother shook her head. "He must have left sometime during the night or early this morning. He's gone now."

The girl gasped.

"Was it all right? For him to drive, I mean?" It was bad enough to have to think about his drinking, but to think of his being out on the highway in that condition was almost more than she could stand. What if he had an accident and killed himself or someone else? What if he was lying in his wrecked car somewhere? He could be dead and they wouldn't even know about it for hours.

But her mother wasn't too concerned about that. "Don't get so shaken up over him, Sandy. He hasn't gone very far. He couldn't have."

"But—"

"He's probably at the motel on the edge of town or at the home of one of his drinking buddies."

Sandy was almost afraid to hope that was true.

"Do you really think so?"

"He's like a cat. He's got nine lives—or is it ninety? You don't have to worry about him. He does a very good job of taking care of himself."

She crossed to the dressing table and sat down. Her hands were trembling and her thin fingers worked nervously. Sandy saw that her mother was more disturbed than she had ever seen her before. She went over to her.

"What is it, Mother?"

Their eyes met.

"What do you mean?"

"What is it that you came in here to tell me this morning?"

Her mother managed a thin smile. "You're more observing than I thought."

Sandy shook off the weak compliment. "Is it about Daddy?" she persisted.

Mrs. Cole nodded. "In a way."

Fearfully the girl waited.

"I don't know exactly how to tell you this, Sandy. I don't even know how to say it so that you will understand."

"I'll try to understand, Mother."

"Thank you, my dear." She grasped her daughter's hand and squeezed it convulsively. "I know that this is going to be as hard for you as it will be for me."

Sandy moistened her lips but did not speak. She wanted to clasp her hand over her mother's mouth to keep her from speaking, so great was her dread of what she was about to say. And yet she had to hear it. She had to know!

"I—I tried to keep Daddy's problem from you as long as I could," Mrs. Cole continued. "I—I even

Divorce 69

lied to you about him because I—I didn't want you to be hurt, but that's no good. I can't keep it up any longer."

Sandy nodded. She had known all about her father's drinking long before her mother had ever mentioned it to her. The times when Mrs. Cole had talked about Daddy being sick hadn't deceived Sandy, but she tried to keep both of them from knowing that she knew the truth.

"You do know that it's been getting worse and worse, don't you?"

"I know." Sandy spoke so softly that her mother had to strain to hear her. Even that admission, however, was difficult for the girl. She, too, had done as much as she could to cover up for her dad.

"I've tried to put up with his drinking all these years, thinking it would get better. But he doesn't even try to control his drinking anymore. He puts liquor ahead of his business and you and me—everything. It's all that matters to him."

Sandy spoke defensively. "Dad told me that he wants to quit and I know that he does. If we only give him the encouragement he needs, he'll quit drinking. I know he will."

Her mother bristled. "You'll soon find out that you can't believe a single word he says."

"But—" That helpless, bewildered look came back to her eyes.

"Sandy," her mother went on. "You might as well

know that I've decided there's no use in fighting anymore. I've got to live my own life with a little bit of happiness."

Sandy moistened her lips with the tip of her tongue. "What do you mean by that, Mother?"

"I mean that I'm through. I've decided to divorce your father!"

Sandy's head reeled. She heard her mother's voice talking about divorce, but it was distant and blurred. It couldn't be true that her parents were separating. That was the sort of thing that happened to other people. She had some friends whose folks were divorced, and she had always felt so sorry for them. This couldn't be happening in her family. In spite of all the problems and trouble there had been at home, this had to be a grim, crude joke. Or maybe it was just a mistake. A mistake that would be straightened out once her mother and dad saw how terribly it was going to affect all three of them. Her folks loved her and each other too much to get a divorce.

Take Daddy, she reasoned. He loved her so much that he would give her anything she wanted, or do anything that he could possibly do. He wouldn't let his drinking separate them. He would quit drinking and come back into their home to be the kind of a father he ought to be.

Yet, she realized that it was happening. Somehow Sandy had known that it would someday—even

Divorce

before her mother came in to break the news to her. She had been fearing this moment for months. Still, just being aware that it was coming did little to ease the hurt.

She looked up to see that her mother was studying her face with something akin to desperation in her eyes. Sandy knew that she should say something. Her mother was waiting for her to tell her that she was as angry with Daddy as she was, that she didn't blame her for wanting to get a divorce, and that she never wanted to see him again. But she couldn't do that!

"Don't look at me that way, Sandy!" her mother cried, her voice defensive and accusing. "I can't put up with your father's drinking and abuse anymore. If I don't sue him for divorce I—I think I'll go out of my mind!"

Sandy pulled away from her mother and moved back to the bed and sat down numbly. She wanted to cry, to sob out the agony that churned so wildly within her. But she could not.

"Will—will we ever see Daddy again?" she wanted to know.

Mrs. Cole choked back the tears. "I don't know why you would want to see him again, after all he's done. He doesn't care anything about us!"

Sandy's eyes widened. "But I care about him!" she exclaimed.

With that Mrs. Cole began to cry bitterly. Her

shoulders shook and the tears streaked the makeup on her face. Sandy, too, began to cry silently. She stared out the window, ignoring her mother. Something within her had withered and died. She felt lifeless, numb to everything that was going on around her.

Presently her mother stopped sobbing and came over to put her arms about Sandy in a clumsy attempt to comfort her. Inwardly Sandy cringed. She wished that her mother wouldn't even touch her. It didn't seem right, now that she had decided to divorce Daddy.

Sandy looked up into her mother's tear-stained face. Instantly she was sorry for her. Her mother had been through a lot, she knew. There were days and nights when she hadn't known where Daddy was, or whether he was alive or dead. And when he would come home, flushed and belligerent, she had to undergo his abuse.

But it had been hard for Daddy too. He had not been drinking because he wanted to, Sandy was sure. He wasn't that kind of a person. He would quit if he could. But liquor had such a hold on him that he didn't seem to be able to control himself. And now, if Mother divorced him, it would be harder than ever for him to lick this thing that had such a grip on him.

Sandy ran a trembling hand across her face. If

Divorce

only she knew what to do! If only she knew which one was right!

That was the trouble. They were both right and they were both wrong. And, as far as she was concerned, they were going to expect her to make a choice. They would expect her to take sides with one or the other. But she didn't want to take sides with either one. She didn't care what they had done or what they hadn't done. She loved them both. She couldn't take sides and shut one of her parents or the other out of her life!

* * *

That same morning Del had something planned. He was going out to the cabin and see Barney. It had been a couple of weeks since he had spent any time with his elderly Cree friend. Barney would be beginning to think there was something wrong, or that he didn't enjoy coming to visit him anymore.

He had breakfast and got his chores done an hour earlier than usual to give him a little more time with Barney. Then he started for the barn to saddle his horse for the ride along the lake, but at the barn door he stopped and went back to the house to ask Doug to join him.

His brother eyed him coldly. "Sorry. I've already got something else to do."

Del squinted questioningly at him. "Going over to see Sandy this morning?"

"Sandy?" Doug was irritated by the remark but

tried not to show it. "Sandy's after you now. Remember?"

"That's what you think. The football season's almost over, and when it is you'll start playing basketball. That's what gets her, the groovy way you move around the floor."

"I saw how she acted a couple of weeks ago. She's after you, and that's for sure."

"When you start sinking those baskets from any old place on the floor, the telephone will start ringing again, and it won't be for me." His laughter trilled. "I can just hear her now. 'I'd like to speak to Douglas, please.'"

Doug's cheeks flushed. "Lay off, will you, Del? That stuff's not funny."

His brother laughed tauntingly.

"You may not think it's funny, but I do. I've seen that look in her eyes. You send her, man. You really send her!"

"I don't know why you have to keep harping on that same old corny stuff. I've about had it."

Del changed the subject quickly. "That isn't why I came back in here. Why don't you ride out to Barney's with me this morning? I haven't seen him for a long time, and neither have you."

Doug seemed to respond to his brother's invitation. "I'd like to, but I already promised Larry Larson that I'd come over and practice basketball

Divorce

in his basement with him. Johnny's going to give us some pointers."

"You mean you're starting to practice basketball already?"

"Mostly we'll just be fooling around, but we do want to be ready when the season opens."

"I'll be back by noon."

"Maybe I can go with you the next time." Doug sounded as though he was disappointed that he wasn't able to go with him to see Barney, but Del couldn't be sure. It just might be an act.

In spite of the warmth in Doug's voice, Del was disappointed as he saddled his horse and led him out of the barn. All Doug was interested in was sports, and especially basketball. It didn't do any good to try to make up with him and spend some time with him. He wouldn't do it unless Del went along with what he wanted to do.

8

Alex's Counseling

AT FIRST Sandy had felt that she could not talk with anyone about the trouble that her parents were having. She couldn't let any of the kids know that they were talking about a divorce. Nobody would understand. Not even DeeDee, who was her very best friend. Danny and Kay Orlis were so religious that she was afraid they probably wouldn't even want DeeDee to associate with her when they found out about it.

Sandy moved to the window, her eyes focusing on the bleak yard. The leaves had died and fallen to the ground, leaving the trees stark and bare against the ashen sky. The lawn was brown and patched with snow, the remnants of an earlier storm. A brief flurry of snow that began that morning gave hint of more to come, and the wind made the temperature seem even colder than it was. But, according to the weather forecast of the day before, it was due to get colder before it warmed up.

Alex's Counseling

But that didn't concern Sandy. Nothing seriously concerned her anymore. Her world, her very life, had ground miserably to a halt.

The chill of that late fall afternoon was as nothing compared to the chill that gripped the distraught girl.

Mother and Daddy couldn't get a divorce. They just couldn't. There had to be some way of stopping them, some way of bringing them to their senses before they did something that would ruin all their lives. But, even as she reasoned angrily with herself regarding it, she knew that there was nothing she could do about it! She had heard that tone in her mother's voice, a tone of finality that was chilling.

Sandy had not moved from the window when her mother came to the living room door. "Sandy, isn't it about time for you to leave for school?"

School? How could she go to school and face the kids with such a burden on her heart?

A lot of the kids probably knew about the coming divorce already. Things like that had a way of spreading in a town like Fairview. When she got to school they would undoubtedly be talking about her behind her back, pretending to feel so sorry for her, but all the time they would be looking down on her. None of them would want to have anything to do with her now.

"Sandy, if you don't hurry, you'll be late for school."

The girl shrugged indifferently. Why should she care? Why should anything matter to her anymore? She wanted to tell her mother that, to inform her coldly that she wasn't going to go to school anymore. But, if she did, she knew that her mother would only start to cry again and make another scene worse than the last one.

"I'm just leaving."

Her mother came into the living room, her eyes searching Sandy's desperately for some sign of understanding and approval.

"I've got to run an errand this morning. I can take you by the school if you'd like me to."

Sandy hesitated. She would rather walk, but she knew how her mother felt about that. "All right, if that's what you want to do."

On the way to school Mrs. Cole talked brightly about many things, as though trying to force thoughts of the pending divorce from both her mind and that of her daughter. She stopped the car in front of the school building.

"I could come by after you, if I know what time you'll be coming home."

"That won't be necessary, Mother. I can walk."

Sandy started to get out of the car, but Mrs. Cole laid a hand impulsively on her arm. "Sandy, please don't feel so terrible toward me. I'm only doing what I've got to do. Don't you understand?"

Their eyes met.

Alex's Counseling

"No, Mother," Sandy retorted icily, "I don't understand. I don't understand at all."

A dry sob constricted her mother's throat, and Sandy cringed. She didn't know why her mother had to say something about the divorce at this particular time—when she had to go into the school building and face the kids. Swallowing hard, she got out of the car and made her way up the steps and into the building.

Fortunately she was early and few of the kids were at school. She brushed past a girl who was on her way to band practice and went into her homeroom. Miss Newton was at her desk, the only one in the room.

"Good morning, Sandy," she said brightly.

She muttered a greeting in return.

"You're here early this morning."

"I know." She sat down and began to fumble with her books. Mother was all upset because she wasn't overjoyed at the idea of a divorce. She wasn't interested in doing anything to salvage their marriage, or even trying to help Daddy. All she could think of was to get rid of him. And she expected Sandy to be happy about that. Tears welled in her eyes and she brushed them quickly away.

She didn't quite know how Miss Newton knew she was disturbed. She had kept her head turned so the teacher couldn't see her tears. But Miss Newton noticed that something was wrong, anyway. She got up and came back to Sandy's desk.

"Sandy, is there something wrong?" She spoke softly, concern edging her voice.

Sandy shook her head, but did not look up.

"Can I help you, Sandy?" the teacher repeated.

Slowly she raised her head. "No!" The word lashed out. "There's nothing you can do! There's nothing anybody can do!"

Miss Newton bent over her. "I don't mean to pry, but there are times when it helps to talk things out, dear." She breathed deeply. "Would you like to tell me what is troubling you so deeply this morning?"

Sandy shook her head. It wouldn't do any good to tell Miss Newton or anyone else. She wouldn't be able to do anything about the problem that troubled her. Nobody could. That was what made it so difficult.

The teacher stood helplessly beside Sandy for a moment or two. She wanted to help lighten the load the girl was obviously carrying, but she didn't know what to say to her.

"The others will be coming in a few minutes, Sandy," she said, her voice gentle. "It might not be so good if they saw you crying. It might start the story that you're having difficulties of some sort, and I wouldn't want to have you hurt by loose talking."

That was something Sandy hadn't thought about

Alex's Counseling

until that moment. She struggled to regain control of herself and stop crying.

She had always liked Miss Newton, but in that moment she thought she liked her better than she ever had. She was genuinely concerned about her as a person. She wasn't just a teacher. She was a friend as well. Sandy straightened in her seat and wiped the last tears from her eyes. Even though she did like her homeroom teacher she didn't feel that she could tell her what was troubling her so much. At that moment she didn't feel that she could tell anyone about it. It was one of those things she would have to keep bottled deeply within her.

"Please forgive me for interfering with something that isn't any of my business," Miss Newton continued, "but you know that we have a counselor at school who is here to help you kids with some of your problems."

She nodded. She knew that Alex Smith was not only the football coach but the guidance counselor as well. He helped kids decide what fields they would be best suited to train for as life's work, but his duties were more than that. He was also on the staff to help kids with problems that were disturbing them, problems that could affect their schoolwork.

"If this matter is something that you would like to talk over with Mr. Smith, I'd be glad to make arrangements for you to see him. I know he'd be willing to counsel with you anytime."

82   *Danny Orlis and the Football Feud*

Sandy hesitated. There just might be some value to talking with someone like Mr. Smith. He might be able to tell her what she could do to get her dad to stop drinking and to keep her parents together.

"I—I think I would like to talk to him," she said uncertainly. "That is, if he—he wouldn't tell anybody about my coming to see him."

Miss Newton smiled reassuringly. "You don't have to worry about that. I'm sure that he won't tell anyone about your visit with him."

Miss Newton left the room and came back a moment or two later. "Mr. Smith says that he'll see you now."

Sandy's eyes widened. "Now?" she echoed. "You mean right away?"

"Yes, you can see him right away. And you won't have to worry about going to your next class. If you and Mr. Smith aren't through talking he will see that you are excused from class."

Sandy made her way mechanically down the hall to the counselor's office. She met DeeDee in the corridor on the way.

"Hi, Sandy," DeeDee sang out brightly.

She spoke and hurried on, conscious of the fact that her friend had stopped and turned to look after her curiously. She slowed her rapid walk until she was sure that her friend had gone into their homeroom. Then she made her way to Alex's office.

He visited with her for a moment or two, putting

Alex's Counseling

her at ease. At last he got to the reason for her visit. "Miss Newton tells me that you've got something that you'd like to talk with me about."

"She—she thought maybe you—you would be able to help me."

"I see." His grin flashed encouragingly. "I'll certainly try."

It was almost a minute before she was able to begin. She swallowed against the lump in her throat and blurted out the first few words of explanation.

"This doesn't have anything to do with school," she said, "so maybe I shouldn't even be talking with you about it."

"It has something to do with you. That means that it's a matter of concern for me."

She almost wished that she hadn't come to him at all, but she had, and she had started to talk with him. She had to continue. She told him about her dad's drinking and her mother's nagging and the trouble there had been at home for the last few months. She thought perhaps Alex would be shocked by it, but he gave no sign that he considered it as anything different than what he heard every day.

". . . And now Mother and Daddy say that they are going to get a divorce." Tears filled her eyes. "And there's nothing I can do about it."

"I'm very sorry to hear that, Sandy. I'm sure it is most difficult for you."

He did understand! She raised her head to look

at him thankfully. And she could tell by the way he talked that his lips would be sealed as far as other people were concerned.

"I—I suppose this sounds silly to you," she went on, "but I keep thinking about this and—and I keep wondering if there's anything I can do to help Daddy stop drinking and to get them to go back together again."

He paused, frowning thoughtfully. "Yes, I can imagine that this is your biggest concern, Sandy. I can sympathize with you. I've talked with other kids who face the same hard problems that you do."

"You have?" Her eyes lighted briefly. She hadn't thought there were any others in all of Fairview who had the same kind of a problem that she had. "And —and what sort of advice do you give them?"

He took a pencil from his pocket and fingered it as he spoke. "First of all, you've got to remember that this isn't the sort of problem you can solve alone. If you were the one who was doing the drinking, or if you were the one who was getting a divorce, you would be in a position to deal directly with the matter. But you're not."

She thought she understood the situation a little better after he explained it that way.

"So, you've got to accept the fact that you're not responsible for what is happening."

That won't be easy to do, she told herself inwardly. Ever since her mother told her about her de-

Alex's Counseling

cision to get a divorce, she had been blaming herself for it.

"Now I do think that you might be able to help your parents to get their thinking straightened out."

"You do?" Sandy's eyes widened hopefully.

"Why don't you talk with them about going to see a marriage counselor?"

The lights in Sandy's eyes dimmed. "They'd never do that."

"They might, if you ask them to."

The more Sandy thought about it, the more excited she became. Her mother kept talking about how badly she felt and how she wanted Sandy to be happy. If she asked her to go to a marriage counselor, she just might do it.

And as far as Daddy was concerned, she could handle him. She knew that he would do it if she asked him to.

Sandy could scarcely wait to get home from school that afternoon to talk with her mother. Mrs. Cole saw that something had happened the moment she came in.

"You act almost happy this afternoon, dear," she said.

"There's something I want to talk with you about." Sandy sat down across from her mother in the huge Cole living room and asked her about going to a marriage counselor.

Her mother's eyes flashed. "And who put you up to that?" she demanded.

"I—I don't know what you mean."

"You wouldn't have thought about a thing like that yourself." Ice wrapped Mrs. Cole's voice. "Did that father of yours put you up to it?"

"I—I haven't seen Daddy," she blurted.

"Somebody has been talking to you."

Sandy swallowed hard. "Will you, Mother?" she pleaded. "Will you?"

"My mind is made up. I don't intend to talk to anybody!"

Sandy's new hopes crashed at her feet.

9
New Insight for DeeDee

SHORTLY AFTER DINNER that evening Sandy went to bed without even helping with the dishes. When her mother asked her about it she informed her that she had had a terrific headache all day.

"I can understand why," Mrs. Cole replied. "I've had a headache most of the time the last three or four weeks. It's that father of yours. He makes everyone miserable who has ever had to be around him."

Sandy's temper surged, but she did not attempt to answer. There was no use in trying to argue with her mother. If she did, she would only start crying again, claiming that Sandy was taking sides against her and with her father. It was no use even trying to talk to her.

She should have known that her mother would not consent to going with her dad to a marriage counselor, even if she could select him herself. After all, she had already made up her mind that her husband was wrong in everything and she was right. Sandy knew that even if her mother did agree to go and talk with someone it probably wouldn't do any good. She wouldn't try to find help for their problems. Instead, she'd only try to justify the things she had done.

Sandy twisted and tossed miserably until morning. When she got up she was as tired and upset as she had been when she went to bed.

It was hard for her to go to school that morning. She was half afraid that Miss Newton would come up and ask her if Mr. Smith had been able to help her with her problem. Or, she thought, Mr. Smith might seek her out and ask her if her folks had agreed to go to a marriage counselor as he had suggested.

Then there were the kids. They might not know about the divorce now, but it wouldn't be long until they would. And when one or two found out, the story would spread all over school, and she wouldn't be able to face any of her friends.

When that happened, she decided, she would leave school. She didn't care what anyone said. She wasn't going to come and have everyone talk about her and ridicule her mother and dad. She'd quit school first.

Sandy talked with DeeDee when she met her in the hall or saw her at noon, but she tried to avoid

New Insight for DeeDee

her if she could. DeeDee wouldn't understand either.

DeeDee was disturbed by the attitude her best friend was showing. She saw that Sandy seldom laughed and her downcast eyes were often reddened. Finally she could bear it no longer and impulsively went up to Sandy and whispered to her in a voice so soft that nobody else could hear what she said.

"Is there anything I can do to help?"

Sandy didn't know why, but DeeDee's gentle question brought tears to her eyes.

"There's nothing that anybody can do," she murmured, her voice flat and expressionless.

There was something her folks could do, she told herself, if they only would. They could go to a marriage counselor and get the problems of their marriage worked out. Daddy could quit drinking and Mother could forgive him and quit nagging at him all the time. They could straighten everything out and go back to living the way they had before—before all of that trouble. But they didn't want to! All they were concerned about was getting a divorce. They didn't care what would happen to themselves or to her.

The two girls walked down the corridor together. Sandy hesitated, glancing around. "I—I can't talk here," she blurted on impulse. Suddenly she felt that she had to talk with DeeDee. She had to tell her everything.

"I'm not very hungry this noon. Why don't we go

for a walk?" DeeDee suggested. Then we can talk without having to be afraid that half the school is overhearing us."

Sandy did not reply, but she allowed her best friend to lead her out of the school building into the chill late fall wind. They ignored the snow that was beginning to sift down, and the shivering cold. For a time they walked in silence until at last Sandy felt that she had control of herself well enough to talk.

"You remember the time that you were at our house and—and Daddy came home drunk, don't you?" she began.

DeeDee nodded. How could she forget that? She had been frightened half out of her mind.

"It's been happening a lot lately," the other girl continued. "Sometimes it seems that—that Daddy is drunk more than he's sober."

"That's too bad. I thought he had promised you that he was going to quit drinking."

"He did. And I know that he really meant it when he promised me that he'd quit. He was almost crying, he felt so bad about it and the way that he had hurt us. He told me that he didn't ever want to do anything that would hurt me and that he wasn't going to drink anymore or gamble or do anything like that. He said that he knew how terribly mean he'd been to Mother and me and he was going to make it up to us. He was going to make us proud of him." Bitterness crept into her voice.

New Insight for DeeDee

"He did quit drinking for a while, didn't he?"

"He quit for a while, but now—"

DeeDee felt so bad about the trouble Sandy was having at home that she was afraid she was going to cry too.

Sandy's voice carried a strangely hysterical note that disturbed DeeDee even more than the things she was saying.

"Like I told you," she continued, "there isn't anything that anyone can do." The words choked in her throat and it was a minute or two before she was able to go on. "You don't know what it's been like around our place. Mother and Daddy haven't been nice to each other one day a month. It seems to me that they try as hard as they can to think of the meanest, nastiest things to say to each other."

DeeDee nodded as though she understood, but she really didn't have any idea what Sandy was saying. She could never remember having heard her parents argue, and it had been the same since she and the boys had come to live with Danny and Kay. Of course they had differences of opinion occasionally over what they should do, but they discussed those differences without ever getting mad. She had never heard Kay say anything mean and spiteful to Danny.

It seemed as though Sandy knew what her companion was thinking. "You don't know how lucky you are to be living with people like Danny and Kay."

"What do you mean?"

"It must be wonderful to live in a home where there isn't fighting all the time, and where the people who live there act as though they really and truly love each other. I don't know what that would be like."

"God sent us to live with Danny and Kay," Dee-Dee told her.

Sandy eyed her quizzically, as though she didn't quite understand what DeeDee meant, but she did not ask about it. Instead, she continued to talk about Danny and Kay and the kind of a home they had.

"I don't think I ever told you this, but when I've been out to visit you, I've almost wished that I could stay there. It's so pleasant that I didn't even want to go home."

The words stabbed deeply into DeeDee's heart. Ever since she had started to run around with Sandy, she had been envious of her and had been critical of almost everything about Danny and Kay. She had been jealous of Sandy's beautiful home and all her fine clothes and the spending money she was given so freely and without ever having to account for it. Also, she had been jealous of the way Sandy's parents let her go anywhere she wanted to and come in whenever she wanted without asking any questions. Often she had thought how good it would be to live

New Insight for DeeDee

in a home like that where she could do as she pleased.

Sandy must have been thinking about the same thing. "You know, my folks don't even love me as much as Danny and Kay love you, and they're my real parents."

DeeDee spoke quickly. "That couldn't be true." There were times when she had resented Danny and Kay for the very fact that they weren't her real parents, and thought she was being taken advantage of for that reason. She couldn't quite understand what her friend was trying to say.

"But it is true." Sandy swallowed at the lump in her throat as her bitterness came surging back. "My parents don't care who I run around with, or where I go, or what I do, or what time I get in. Daddy never asks me anything about my friends. He doesn't even warn me to be careful of the kids I associate with." She paused and breathed deeply. "I've been out to your place and Danny always wants to know everything about you." A wistful tone crept into her voice. "He must really love you or he wouldn't care so much about what happens to you."

Tears flooded DeeDee's eyes. She had never looked at it that way before. She had always thought of Danny's interest as interference. Now, she realized, she was seeing it as it really was. She was so ashamed of her attitude she didn't think she could stand it.

The noon hour was almost up before the girls returned to the school. Sandy was afraid she couldn't go in and sit through classes the rest of the day.

"You don't want to stay away from school," DeeDee told her. "I'll pray for you."

Once she had spoken she eyed her friend narrowly. She had seldom ever said anything like that to Sandy. She really hadn't meant to. She was so concerned for her friend that the words slipped out. Now she wondered if she had made Sandy angry.

"Thank you, DeeDee," Sandy murmured. It was obvious that she meant it. DeeDee was thankful for that.

Outside their homeroom Sandy paused briefly.

"You won't say anything about this to anyone, will you?" she asked. "If anyone else finds out what I've just told you I—I'll just die!"

DeeDee shook her head. "You won't have to worry about my telling anyone. I won't let anyone else know what you've just shared with me. You can count on it."

DeeDee tried hard to keep her mind on her lessons the rest of the afternoon, but every time she looked in her book Sandy's sad face swam on the page before her. She wished there was something she could do for her friend—something that would give her strength and assurance that things would work out all right in the end.

She wished that Sandy hadn't asked her to keep

New Insight for DeeDee

the matter a secret. She would have felt better if she could share the problem with Kay. Danny and Kay would pray about it. They might even have some sort of a solution for the problem that was so disturbing to Sandy. But, as it was, DeeDee couldn't tell them anything. She couldn't violate the confidence that Sandy put in her. And so, as she tried to study, she prayed silently for her friend.

* * *

Del continued to set a torrid pace on the football field. He scored the winning touchdowns in the next two games and set up the field goal that nosed out the opposition with a long run in the dying moments of the third game. For the first time in a number of years the Fairview team was within two victories of a perfect season.

Alex Smith called his squad together before the next contest. "I'm sure you fellows realize exactly what we have at stake this evening. If we can get by Mobridge, we have one more game between us and an undefeated season."

Two or three fellows grinned confidently. Mobridge wasn't the toughest competition they could meet by far. They had tied two games and lost three, one by a sizable score.

"I know you're thinking about Mobridge's record," Alex continued, "but don't let that fool you. They've got a better team than their win-loss record would indicate. And if we don't stay on top of the situation every minute, we're going to get clobbered." With that he turned slowly to Del. "How about it? Are you ready?"

Doug winced. What was the matter with Coach Smith anyway? Didn't he know there were going to be ten other guys on the field besides Del? If it wasn't for the blocking he got, he couldn't make the long runs and score the way he had been doing.

As they trotted out to the football field, Del edged over to his brother. "How about it, Doug? Are *you* ready for today's game?" He deliberately used the words the coach had used.

Doug glared at him in silence. He'd show him! When they got out on the field he'd show him what kind of a player he was.

As Alex had said, Mobridge had a better team than the scores of their earlier games indicated. They had a strong pass defense and a line that was as stubborn and unyielding as Fairview faced all year. Even Doug had to admit that Del made the difference. He wasn't able to break free for any long runs, but he consistently knocked off yardage, punching the ball from the Fairview thirty-two-yard line to the Mobridge eleven before Larry Larson faked a handoff to him and knifed across for the touchdown.

In the fourth quarter after Mobridge came roaring back to tie the score, Del took a short screen pass from Larry to set up the field goal that won the game.

New Insight for DeeDee

The players were grinning broadly as they trotted off the field. "One more to go," Larry said happily. "One more win and we'll do it! We'll sweep the board clean!"

Doug's scowl deepened. They all had a part in what had happened that season, but not according to Del. As far as he was concerned he acted as though he had done it all single-handedly.

10

Passing the Buck

DANNY HAD SEEN the trouble building between Del and Doug, especially in the day following the Mobridge game. The boys scarcely spoke to each other, and when they did, their voices were cold and belligerent. He knew that he was going to have to talk with them.

When Danny came into the house that afternoon he found Doug in the living room alone.

"Hi, Doug. Is Del around?"

Doug's laughter was more like a sneer. "He went out in the woods to try to find that pet deer of his to see how he's getting along. He wanted me to go along, but I told him I've got some more important things to do."

"Jumper is very important to Del," Danny reminded him quietly.

"I know, but it's no reason why I have to buy that. I tried to tell him that it's a waste of time trying to

Passing the Buck

play nursemaid to a deer as big as Jumper is now. He can take care of himself without help from Del or anybody, but Del won't pay any attention to anything I say."

With that the boy started into the other room, but Danny stopped him. "Are you in a big hurry?"

Doug turned back reluctantly. "I guess not. Why?"

"If you've got a few minutes, there's something that I'd like to talk with you about."

Something about Danny's tone sobered the boy. "Have I done something I shouldn't have?"

"Not exactly."

Doug sighed. "I'm glad of that. For a minute I I thought I was going to get the third degree."

Danny shook his head. "Oh, now, it's nothing like that. I want to talk with you about Del."

He stiffened noticeably. "What about him?"

"You guys haven't been getting along very well lately, have you?"

Doug's cheeks darkened. "You're talking to the wrong guy this time. Del's the one who won't get along with me. I've tried and tried to get things back to the way they used to be, but it doesn't do any good, Danny. To tell you the truth, he's got the big head. People started making over him a little because he's been lucky on the football field and he thinks he's the greatest ballcarrier that ever scored a touchdown."

Danny eyed him obliquely. He rather imagined there was something like this behind it. "You've got to admit that Del's good," he said. "He's one of the few natural broken-field runners I've ever seen."

"But he's not as good as *he* thinks he is," Doug blurted. "Ever since he made the team it's all he can talk about. He wants to tell you about every step of every run he's made, and he can tell you to the foot how much yardage he's gained. Do you know that he's keeping a scrapbook, Danny? A scrapbook filled with pictures and stories about himself."

"I did the same thing when I was in high school," Danny told him.

"But you were never as conceited as he is. I know that much."

There was a short silence.

"I hadn't noticed that he was as conceited as all that, but then I haven't been paying much attention to that." Danny lowered his voice. "If Del is conceited, there's nothing you can do about that. But I think you should seriously ask yourself if you may not be jealous of him."

Doug winced. "Me jealous of Del? Why would I be jealous? He isn't *that* good!"

"Jealousy is one of the things that can cause a great deal of trouble, especially between brothers where there's some natural rivalry anyway."

"Well, you can forget that stupid idea." Doug's

Passing the Buck

eyes blazed. "I was the one who kept after him and after him to get him to go out for football. If I was so jealous of him, why would I do that?"

Danny paused thoughtfully. "Whatever the reason for it, Doug, it's something that hadn't ought to be. As brothers you should stand together. As Christians and brothers, you ought to love each other so much that you rejoice over the accomplishments of each other."

Doug got to his feet. "There's trouble between Del and me," he acknowledged, "that's true. But it's not my fault. Del is the one you ought to be talking to. We'd be getting along great if he didn't have the bighead because he's been lucky this football season. You're talking to the wrong guy."

"Don't worry. I plan to talk with Del too. In fact, I hoped to get you together this afternoon so we could try to get this thing straightened out. It's not right for two Christian brothers to be so belligerent toward each other."

That seemed to please Doug. He sat down once more and leaned back in the chair. "Don't think that I'm jealous of Del because he happened to get a little lucky in a couple of football games or so. Don't forget, I play football too, and the coach says I'm one of the best blockers on the team. So I don't have anything to be jealous about."

"I hope you aren't jealous of Del," Danny continued. "Actually, you have fine athletic ability, and especially as a basketball player. I suppose when it gets right down to it, you're as good on the basketball floor as Del is carrying a football. You each have different talents, just as I have different talents than Ron or Jim Morgan or almost anyone else you can name. Neither you nor Del should be jealous of each other."

Danny went on to explain the spiritual implications of jealousy and trouble between him and Del, and the need for harmony if they were to live consistent Christian lives.

"This is the sort of thing that Satan can use to cause all sorts of problems between you and to be a real hindrance to your testimonies."

Doug saw Del approaching the house and got to his feet quickly. "Like I said, Danny," he replied, "you'd better talk to Del about these things. He's the one who's been causing all the trouble."

As the back door opened, Doug started for his room. "I've got some American history to study."

He went into the bedroom and closed the door behind him. At his desk he picked up his history book and opened it, but he couldn't bring himself to study—at least for the moment.

Del had come in now, but Doug didn't suppose Danny would talk to him. He never seemed to go to Del about anything that involved both boys. He picked on Doug, and Doug couldn't understand why.

Passing the Buck

And, like today, most of the time Danny didn't talk to the real troublemaker.

He couldn't help it that Del was so conceited about his football-playing ability that he figured he had won every game single-handed. And he couldn't help it that Del wouldn't go out for basketball, or that he preferred to play around with a tame crow and that pet deer of his rather than doing the things most guys enjoyed doing.

Doug snorted his indignation. Del thought he was quite a football player, but just wait until they played Norman or somebody else who had a top-drawer team. He'd find out that he wasn't nearly as good as he had been telling everybody he was.

The more Doug thought about his brother, the more his own temper soared. He couldn't figure out why Danny had to talk to him first. Why didn't he place the blame where it really belonged? Del was the one who was causing all the trouble between them. If Danny wanted to put a stop to it, he ought to corner Del about his attitude. Then they could get someplace.

* * *

Danny called Del into the living room and talked with him, going over the same things that he had with Doug.

"Actually, it's all Doug's fault," Del alibied. "He's so jealous of me because I've been able to do fairly well at football that he can hardly stand it."

"He seems to feel that you're conceited, Del, and that you brag all the time."

Del's eyes widened and a deep red stained his cheeks. "Me, conceited?" he echoed. "He's all mixed up, Danny. I've kidded him a little because I know how jealous he is over my football playing, but that's all there is to it. I could quit playing football tomorrow and it wouldn't bother me a bit. I couldn't care less."

"I'm glad you're playing, Del, and it thrills me to see that you're able to do so well at it. But the hard feelings that have come between you and Doug are of real concern to Kay and me." He went on to tell him how much it hurt their Christian testimony. "As believers, we're supposed to be examples to others who don't know Christ as their Saviour. And the way you and Doug have been acting is certainly no example to anyone. The way things are between you and Doug right now I can't imagine any non-Christian looking at you—either of you—and wanting to have what you have."

Del was fuming when he went out to take care of his horse some time later. He didn't know what was the matter with Danny that he would believe a preposterous story like the one Doug handed him. Anyone who knew them could see that Doug's jealousy was the only thing that caused the barrier between them. That, and the fact that whenever they were together, Doug had to be the one who decided what

Passing the Buck

they did, where they went, and when they would get back. As long as he was the boss, everything was great. If Del had an idea of his own, he was conceited. As far as he was concerned, he'd had it. He didn't care what Doug did, he wasn't going to give in to him. Let him go his own way. That was what he wanted, anyhow.

* * *

DeeDee did a great deal of thinking about what Sandy had said to her about her own home and the one Danny and Kay were providing for her and the boys. She had resented their telling her what to do and felt that they were always far too strict, but that was because she had never stopped to think about why they were so careful about whom she was with and the places she went and the time she got in.

Now that she considered it, she saw that it was their concern for her and the kind of persons she and the boys would grow up to be, that caused them to be so careful about what they permitted them to do. Suddenly she was desperately ashamed of the way she had acted. She realized that she must have seemed terribly ungrateful to them.

That night DeeDee started to kneel to ask God's forgiveness but stopped after a halting sentence or two. She remembered hearing Pastor Reeves say that if a person had wronged someone else, they should go to that person first and make things right. Then there would be time to ask God's forgiveness.

She didn't suppose that it made a great deal of difference which was done first, but she was overwhelmed by the need to talk with Danny and Kay immediately. They were already in their bedroom and were probably asleep, but she knocked on the door.

Danny answered.

"Are you still awake?"

"We are now."

"I'm sorry." There was a tremor in her voice as though she was about to cry.

Kay broke in. "Did you want something?"

"I—I'd like to talk to you."

"Sure thing," Danny replied. A moment later he came out of the bedroom, tying the sash on his robe. Kay followed a moment or two later.

"Is there something wrong?" Kay asked.

"No—not the way you're thinking. I—I've just got to talk to you, though. I know I shouldn't have gotten you up tonight, but I—I—" She could no longer speak.

Danny read the concern in her face. "We don't mind getting up," he said gently. But then, when it came to DeeDee, he was usually gentler than with the boys. He realized that she was much more sensitive and tried to be careful in the way he talked to her. "Let's go in and sit down where we can be comfortable."

They went into the living room and found chairs.

Passing the Buck

Danny and Kay expected DeeDee to tell them what was troubling her and waited for her to speak. But she was silent, suddenly stricken dumb. At last Danny spoke.

"Now, DeeDee, what is it that you want to talk to us about?"

She cleared her throat. "I—I don't know exactly how to say this, but I—I want to tell you how sorry I am for the way I've acted the past few months."

Danny and Kay eyed her curiously.

"I'm not sure that I know what you're trying to tell us, DeeDee," Kay finally said. "Is it something that we don't know about?"

Now that DeeDee had begun to talk she had to keep on, telling them everything that was on her heart. "I—I've been so ashamed of our home and the clothes you bought me and—and the way you have made me be so careful about spending money. I—" Her voice choked until she had difficulty in going on.

Danny and Kay waited patiently without commenting. They both knew that DeeDee was having a difficult time confessing to them and they wanted to make it as easy on her as they could.

"I've wished so many times that I could have a house like Sandy lives in and have all the clothes I wanted and never have to account to you or anybody for the places I went or what time I got in."

Kay nodded understandingly. "I know just exactly how you've felt. I had the same sort of problems at times when I was a girl."

DeeDee smiled gratefully. Somehow it made it easier for her to go on, knowing that Kay had faced the same temptations as she had been facing.

"But that's not all. I've gotten so angry at you so many times when I shouldn't have. I know now that you have only been strict with us because you want us to grow up to be good, consistent-living Christians."

Danny broke the silence that followed.

"You're right about that, DeeDee. It would be easier for us to let you and Del and Doug do just as you please, rather than laying down rules and asking you to abide by them. We could save ourselves a lot of concern by letting you make all of your own decisions, but we know that our parents didn't raise us that way and your parents wouldn't have wanted you to be raised that way, and it certainly wouldn't be pleasing to the Lord. I guess the simplest way to explain how we feel is to tell you that we try to discipline you the way we would if you were our own children."

"You are our own children, you know," Kay reminded the girl, "even though you don't bear our name and we didn't bring you into the world. And we are concerned about you."

DeeDee went on. "I—I suppose I'll get mad at you again sometime if I want to do something and

Passing the Buck 109

you tell me not to, but I just want you to know that I'm not really angry about it. I mean, it's sort of good to know that you do care enough about us to want us to be good, consistent Christians."

Impulsively, she went over and kissed them. Danny looped his arm about her and held her momentarily. "You don't know how happy it makes us feel to have you come and talk to us this way, DeeDee. We've sensed your attitude, and you'll remember that both Kay and I have talked with you about it several times."

She nodded. "I said I was sorry, but to be real honest, I don't think I was. At least not the way I am now."

"This is what we've been praying would happen," Kay said.

DeeDee moved as though to go back to her room, but stopped and came back hesitantly. "There—there is something else I'd like to talk to you about."

"Yes?"

"I—I can't tell you what it is because I promised a—a friend of mine that I wouldn't let anyone know what she confided in me. But, she—she's got a terrible problem at home and I—I'd appreciate it if you would pray for her and her parents."

Danny and Kay both assured her that they would. "Why don't we begin by praying about it right now?"

Bowing his head, Danny asked God to work in

the lives of the people DeeDee was so concerned about. "We don't know who these people are, Lord, and it doesn't matter. You know them and what their problem is. You know what it is that's bothering this friend of DeeDee's. We pray that You will work it out in Your own way, and that You will protect and take care of this person. And, if she isn't a Christian, may she come to the place where she will put her trust in You."

DeeDee kissed them each again and returned to her room. When she knelt it was not only to ask God's forgiveness but to thank Him again for Danny and Kay and the way they watched over her and the boys. It gave her a strong sense of security and trust to know that they were concerned about her future and were praying for her and guiding her.

It was possible for her to go wrong. She knew that happened to Christian kids all the time. Yet, it would be so much easier to go the right way with Danny and Kay to help her.

11

Another Chance

HALFWAY ACROSS TOWN at the Cole home, Sandy's parents were sitting in the living room glaring belligerently at each other. Mrs. Cole's eyes snapped and scorn rasped in her voice.

"It isn't going to do a bit of good for you to plead with me. I've made up my mind." All the bitterness of the past few months welled up within her. "I've had all I can take. I'm tired of trying to get you to quit drinking. I'm tired of fighting."

"So am I." His tone was conciliatory.

"You don't understand. I'm done! Finished! I'm going to divorce you!" Venom dripped from her words. "And nothing you can say will talk me out of it!"

Surprisingly, he did not argue with her.

"I don't blame you for wanting a divorce. I know I don't deserve anything else after the way I've treated you and Sandy all these years. But I want you to know that I've had it too. I'm going to quit drinking."

There was a long, painful silence during which they only stared at one another. At last Mrs. Cole spoke once more.

"This isn't the way I want it, believe me. But it's no use. I can't go through anymore. I think I'll go mad if I have to. I've got to give up. There isn't any use in trying to patch things up between us. Too much has happened the past months for there to be any love left for you."

He got to his feet unsteadily, running a trembling hand through his hair. "Like I said, I don't blame you at all for feeling the way you do. I've done everything I shouldn't do and very few things that I should. But I want you to know that in spite of all of that, I do love you and Sandy very much."

At the mention of their daughter, Mrs. Cole started to cry. Tears had come often during the past few weeks. It was some time before she could speak again.

"You probably don't know this. You haven't been sober enough lately to find out anything about either Sandy or me, but she's been so upset since I told her that we were getting a divorce that she's scarcely been able to eat or sleep, and I know she hasn't been able to study. To tell you the truth, I'm concerned that her grades will drop to failing this semester."

Another Chance

Mr. Cole winced as though she had struck him in the face. "You must be mistaken," he mumbled. "Sandy's a good student. She always has been."

"The trouble is, she doesn't care what happens to her now. I've never seen her the way she's been these past few days. It frightens me."

The girl's father nodded.

"I know just how she feels. I've felt the same way."

Mrs. Cole dabbed at her eyes once more. "It hasn't been easy for me, either.

He turned and grasped her shoulders with his hands. "We don't have to go through with this, you know. We don't have to get a divorce."

She did not speak immediately, but when she did her voice was flat and expressionless, devoid of strength.

"It's no use. I'm tired of hoping and trusting and being disappointed. I'm tired of fighting. I'm so sick of the whole rotten mess I—I—" The tears came once more.

His voice was so low she could scarcely hear it. "I don't suppose it will help any to say I'm sorry."

Sobbing, she buried her head in her arms. He sat on the divan beside her and put his arm around her tenderly. "Now, look." His voice was gentle and conciliatory. She hadn't heard him use that tone in years. "You don't want a divorce and I don't want one. In addition to that, it's breaking our daughter's heart. Why don't we try again?"

She stopped crying and looked up. "It wouldn't be any use."

"But it would! We still love each other. We could build a happy home. We don't have to go on like this. I promise you that I'll quit drinking. I'll do anything you say, only don't go through with this divorce."

She hesitated.

"You've promised to quit drinking before."

"But I've never felt about it the way I do right now." His voice rose for emphasis. "You won't have to worry about liquor. If you'll just take me back, I'll promise you that things will be the way they were when we were first married. I'll never take another drink as long as I live!"

Mrs. Cole was a minute or more in answering. "When I was talking to Sandy a day or so ago she suggested that we go to a marriage counselor and see if we can get some help from him. What would you think of that?"

Her husband scowled. "What can a guy like that know about our problems?"

"If you mean what you're saying just now, you ought to be willing to go to someone and get some professional help."

"We're the ones who have to work things out. I don't see what anyone else can do about it."

Another Chance

She drew herself erect. "If you aren't serious enough about reforming to go with me to get some counseling guidance, we'll just forget it."

"Oh, I'll go with you," he said quickly. "I'll go with you anyplace you want to go."

"And you'll try to follow his suggestions, so we can get our marriage to the place where it ought to be?"

"I'll not only try to follow his suggestions, I'll follow them. I guarantee it."

She squirmed nervously. "If I could just trust you."

He took her in his arms. "You can trust me now. I've got something to stay sober for." Sincerity rang in his voice.

For an hour or more after that they sat in the living room, talking about things they hadn't mentioned in years. They scarcely realized that half the night was gone when they finally started upstairs to bed.

"I think I'm going to stop and tell Sandy," Mrs. Cole said.

"She's probably asleep by this time. Shouldn't you wait until morning?"

She shook her head. "I want to tell her now."

"That's all right with me. Want me to be with you when you talk to her?"

"I don't think so. I—I'd rather talk to her alone."

She knocked on their daughter's door. The girl jerked awake instantly.

"Sandy!"

She did not answer.

"Sandy!" This time her mother called loudly. "I'd like to talk to you."

"Come on in. I'm awake."

Mrs. Cole came into the room and sat on the side of the bed. "Daddy thought I should wait until morning to talk to you, but I decided to wake you up tonight. I hope you don't mind."

Sandy stiffened. Maybe they were going to have to move out in the morning. Maybe—

"Daddy and I had a long talk tonight. We've decided to take your advice and go to a marriage counselor to see what help we can get."

At first Sandy could not believe what her mother was saying. There had to be some mistake!

"You—you mean—"

"That's right. Daddy agreed to go to a marriage counselor with me, and I've agreed not to file for divorce. I'm going to give him one last chance."

Sandy stared incredulously at her mother. "Do you mean it?" she exclaimed. "Do you really and truly mean it?"

"He is so sincere this time that I believe he really wants to get our marriage straightened out. I'm confident that this time he's going to be able to make it!"

Another Chance

"Oh, Mother!" Sandy tried to keep control of herself, but she could not. She burst into tears.

She lay awake most of the night thinking about the wonderful thing that had happened. Daddy and Mother weren't going to get a divorce after all! They were going to a marriage counselor and get their differences worked out. Daddy had promised to quit drinking and they were going to see a marriage counselor so they could get their problem solved and be like other families again.

She could scarcely wait until morning to tell DeeDee the wonderful thing that had happened.

The next day, DeeDee was not the first person she saw. Instead, she met Alex Smith in the corridor just outside his office.

"Hello, Sandy."

Her smile was warm and relaxed.

"You act happy. Are things better in regard to that problem you shared with me?"

Tears of gratitude flooded her eyes. "Oh, yes. And things are just working out wonderfully."

"That's fine. I'm so glad to hear it." He went into his office and closed the door. It was that sort of thing that made his job as a counselor seem worthwhile. Now if the football team could just knock off Dinsmore, everything would be great!

12

Victory

THE FOOTBALL TEAM worked harder to prepare for the last game than they had worked all season. Alex Smith and McKenzie surprised them by making them spend two nights in bruising scrimmage and an extra evening session going over a series of plays they had worked on from time to time all season, but had never used until now.

"This is our last game," Alex began, looking from one to the other of the players just before the game. "We're one victory away from a perfect season."

The fellows nodded solemnly. They had all been thinking about that during the week. And how could they help it, with the coach's signs in the dressing room to remind them.

"We're going into this game with Dinsmore at full strength, and we're going to give them everything we've got." He paused significantly. "If we don't, we're going to have a blot on our season's record."

Victory

Doug grimaced. He hoped that Del was listening to what the coach said about being at full strength. That showed he was thinking about the contribution each man on the squad could make. But he didn't suppose Del had even heard what Coach Smith told them. He usually only heard what he wanted to hear. Maybe tonight he'd find out how important it was for the ballcarrier to have the help of the whole team. Maybe he'd learn what it was like to not have any blocking when he needed it.

"All right," Alex said, glancing at the clock. "It's time for us to get out on the field. Let's go! And everybody hustle!"

Fairview won the toss and elected to receive. The kickoff was a long one, straight into the end zone, and there was no chance for a runback. On the first play Larry Larson, who was the starting quarterback, faked a hand-off to Del and made six yards over tackle. The next play was a pass that gained a first down and put the ball on the fifty-yard line. That was the situation when Larry called for Del to carry the ball.

The play was a fake to the fullback who was to come up fast and dive over the line between tackle and guard as though he had the ball. Del was to hide it as best he could in the crook of his arm, and follow Doug, who was to run interference for him. It was a simple play but it had been good for some of his longest gains on previous occasions. Moreover, it was a play he liked. For some reason he had been able to execute it with precision.

On this occasion it went better than ever. Larry took the pass from center, thrust the ball toward the charging fullback, and tucked it under Del's arms so quickly most of the spectators didn't realize where the ball was. Del moved out fast to follow Doug around end. His brother heard him coming up at top speed at the same time as a tackler charged in.

Doug could have gotten him. It wouldn't have been an easy block, but he could have gotten him if he had really wanted to. As it was, he felt the tackler hit him at an angle and squirm by to clobber Del for a ten-yard loss. A groan went up from the crowd.

Del was slow in getting to his feet. Doug noted that with a measure of satisfaction. That ought to let that great ballcarrier brother of his know there were some other guys on the field who deserved a little credit.

"We'll try that play again." Larry's voice was decisive.

"After a loss like *that?*"

"They won't expect us to come back with the same play this time. We'll fool 'em!"

This time every move functioned even more perfectly than before. Dinsmore was caught flat-footed, expecting a pass. Doug, however, was deliberate. He changed his direction slightly as the tackler

Victory

blasted in. Not enough to be noticeable to anyone on the sidelines. At least he hoped that it wouldn't be noticeable. But it was enough to let the tackler get his hands on Del, slamming him to the ground for a four-yard loss.

"What's the matter with you, Doug?" Del spoke in an undertone, but his brother heard him clearly. "You could have taken that guy out for me if you'd wanted to."

"So, you've got troubles." Doug smirked knowingly at him. "If the great runner gets clobbered a couple of times in a row, it's got to be the fault of somebody else. It couldn't possibly be that Del Davis isn't as great as everybody thinks he is, now could it?"

Del glared at him and growled under his breath. "Just keep your mouth shut and do your own job. That's all I ask of you."

"That's all *you* ask! Big deal!"

They went into the huddle and Larry called the only play possible with the situation fourth and twelve. He got off a good punt which Dinsmore covered on the sixteen-yard line. The Fairview defensive line held the visitors to six yards and Dinsmore kicked. This time Doug took the punt on his own twenty-eight and twisted and squirmed to the thirty-nine-yard line.

Larry Larson took the ball on the next play and

was smeared after a gain of three yards. In the huddle he glanced at Del and barked out a number.

Doug groaned. "Not him again! Not the great all-American!"

Larry repeated the call decisively and left the huddle before either Del or Doug could say more. Anger glinted in Del's eyes as they lined up.

If he had a blocking back he could depend on in this game, things would be different, he reasoned. Nobody could be expected to run without some support. And Doug had let the tacklers nail him both times. He had all but admitted as much.

That was the thing that made Del so furious. It would be bad enough if Doug couldn't do any better, but at least there would be some excuse for it. But he could. He was as good at blocking as anybody on the team. And that made everything worse.

Del wished that they'd let Doug carry the ball just once so he could let a tackler slip through and give him a taste of his own medicine.

Del was so concerned about Doug's failure to block for him and so determined to make good yardage without him that he jumped forward an instant before the ball was snapped. The red flag went down and the whistle shrilled.

"Illegal procedure," the referee called.

Doug taunted his brother under his breath as they lined up five yards behind the former line of scrimmage. "Calm down, all-American! You're getting

Victory 123

as jumpy as a cat. What's the matter? You aren't making the yardage tonight that you usually do. Have you lost your touch?"

Del said nothing. Sweat moistened his forehead and his hands were trembling. He'd show Doug whether he could play football or not. If he wouldn't block for him, he'd make a touchdown without him. He'd show everybody that he didn't have to depend on Doug to do a good job of runinng.

He was supposed to take the hand-off from Larry on the next play, but he was so anxious to be away that he was running before he had a good grip on the ball. It slipped out of his hands and Dinsmore recovered. Del was white and shaken as he went off the field. Alex Smith only glanced at him and Del cringed. He knew what the coach and everyone else was thinking. They thought he had a swelled head from all the publicity he had been getting and was letting them down.

But it wasn't his fault, he stormed inwardly. That stupid brother of his had caused all the trouble. He didn't know why Alex Smith and the others weren't aware of it. Why did they have to blame him for what had happened when it was all Doug's fault?

Dinsmore scored three plays later. They seemed to get the spark they needed from that touchdown and at half time they were ahead 18-0. Dejected, Del walked off the field, his head down.

In the locker room Alex had the team sit down.

He paced back and forth in front of them. For two or three minutes he said nothing. At last he stopped.

"Apparently you fellows don't care to win." His voice iced. "And if you don't, I don't see why I should. The honor of a perfect season would have been yours." He breathed deeply. "Doug, what is the matter with you fellows tonight?"

Doug colored deeply and shrugged his shoulders as though he didn't know what the coach was talking about.

"I thought at first that you were just playing against fellows who were too quick for you, and that was the reason they were sifting through and spilling Del for such big losses. But on the last play of the half, I got a little better angle on the play." Anger tightened his voice. "You deliberately let that man through to smear your brother!"

Doug licked his lips and glanced uneasily from one teammate to the other.

"Shower and dress, Doug," Alex continued. "You're not playing football for me again!"

His face went ashen and desperation gleamed in his eyes.

"I—"

"I can't understand how a brother could do what you've done," the coach said. "You are responsible for the 18-0 score we face. Our defeat tonight is directly and solely because of you!"

Victory

Hostility glittered in the faces of the rest of the squad.

Del stared at Doug. He ought to feel good about what had happened. Doug had gotten what was coming to him. Del had known from the second play of the game that his brother was deliberately missing his assignments so he would look bad. He ought to find real satisfaction in that.

But he didn't. Doug's dismissal was a shock that set Del to thinking more clearly.

For the first time since the football season started, he saw the situation as it really was. Doug may have been jealous of him. He probably was. But Del had not tried to alleviate it. In fact, he had done everything he could to make things worse.

And he had been conceited. He had tried to make himself believe he hadn't been. And he tried to make Danny and the others believe he was modest too. But Doug was close enough to him to read what was actually in his heart.

True, Doug had let the tacklers get to him, but Del knew that he was the real fault of the trouble.

He understood, too, what Danny had been trying to tell him that day he talked with him about the rift between him and Doug and how it hurt their testimonies. And he had been professing to be so concerned about the souls of the guys he played football with! That, too, was only a dodge—a front he had put on to make Christian people believe he was so much more interested in Christian things than the average believer his age. All of this because he was thinking of himself as a football hero.

Suddenly he knew what he had to do.

"Coach, can I say something?" As he spoke he got to his feet.

Every eye in the room was staring fixedly at him.

"If it's important."

Del cleared his throat. "I know you blame Doug for what happened out there tonight," he began, motioning in the direction of the football field with his hand. "And I suppose the rest of you blame him too. But it isn't his fault. It's mine!"

Someone gasped.

By now he had gone so far he had to continue. "I've been so conceited because of the way I've been able to run with the ball that I've forgotten that there were ten other guys on the field helping me. I made fun of Doug every chance I got and tormented him so much that he started to get back at me." He pulled in a deep breath. "I forgot the school, the team and the coach. It's my fault that we're behind 18-0. I'm the one who ought to be sent to the shower and kicked off the team."

A taut silence followed.

"Will you forgive me?"

For a time no one spoke. Then Doug got to his feet.

"It's not all Del's fault," he began. "I was so

Victory

jealous of him that I—I deliberately lay down on the job. So it's my fault too. I need to ask your forgiveness. And yours, too, Del."

Impulsively Del strode over to Doug and extended his hand. If there were tears in his eyes nobody noticed them.

"Please forgive me, Doug. I haven't been the kind of a brother or fellow Christian that I should have been."

Alex Smith went over to them and put his arms around them. "I'm proud of you two. Now, let's go out there and get those eighteen points back. We've got a ball game to win."

Del and Doug lingered in the dressing room for a moment after the others had gone back to the football field.

"It's great to have things squared off between us, isn't it?" Doug said.

"You bet it is. And with God's help, we're never going to let anything like that come between us again."

Del felt like a new person as he took his place in the lineup at the beginning of the third quarter, and so did Doug. He was sure of that. On the first play after the kickoff, Doug threw a block that sprung Del through the line for a nine-yard gain.

A cry went up from the crowd.

For the next two quarters the entire team came alive. In seven plays Fairview scored their first TD, and made the extra point. Two minutes later they recovered a Dinsmore fumble to set up the second score, and midway in the fourth quarter they scored again to give them a three-point lead. As the gun sounded ending the game, Alex Smith grinned broadly.

They'd done it! A perfect season his first year of coaching! Not bad! If he could keep that up he'd build himself a reputation.

Doug and Del had momentarily forgotten the big victory. Arms looped about each other's shoulders, they made their way to the dressing room. Neither of them was listening to what the fans were saying as they made their way to the school.